Mastering Arabic Vocabulary and Pronunciation

Jane Wightwick and Mahmoud Gaafar

Illustrations by Mahmoud Gaafar

BLOOMSBURY ACADEMIC
LONDON • NEW YORK • OXFORD • NEW DELHI • SYDNEY

BLOOMSBURY ACADEMIC

Bloomsbury Publishing Plc, 50 Bedford Square, London, WC1B 3DP, UK
Bloomsbury Publishing Inc, 1385 Broadway, New York, NY 10018, USA
Bloomsbury Publishing Ireland, 29 Earlsfort Terrace, Dublin 2, D02 AY28, Ireland

BLOOMSBURY, BLOOMSBURY ACADEMIC and the Diana logo are trademarks of Bloomsbury Publishing Plc

First published in Great Britain by Palgrave, 4 Crinan Street, London N1 9XWS
First edition 2018
Reprinted by Bloomsbury Academic 2022, 2023, 2024, 2025

Copyright © g-and-w publishing 2005

Jane Wightwick and Mahmoud Gaafar have asserted their rights under the Copyright, Designs and Patents Act, 1988, to be identified as Authors of this work.

All rights reserved. No part of this publication may be: i) reproduced or transmitted in any form, electronic or mechanical, including photocopying, recording or by means of any information storage or retrieval system without prior permission in writing from the publishers; or ii) used or reproduced in any way for the training, development or operation of artificial intelligence (AI) technologies, including generative AI technologies. The rights holders expressly reserve this publication from the text and data mining exception as per Article 4(3) of the Digital Single Market Directive (EU) 2019/790.

Bloomsbury Publishing Plc does not have any control over, or responsibility for, any third-party websites referred to or in this book. All internet addresses given in this book were correct at the time of going to press. The author and publisher regret any inconvenience caused if addresses have changed or sites have ceased to exist, but can accept no responsibility for any such changes.

A catalogue record for this book is available from the British Library.

ISBN PB: 978-1-352-00225-6

Series: Bloomsbury Master Series (Languages)

For product safety related questions contact productsafety@bloomsbury.com.

To find out more about our authors and books visit www.bloomsbury.com and sign up for our newsletters.

Contents

Introduction 1

Unit 1 Sounds and basic words 1 2
        Part 1: Core vocabulary 2
        Part 2: Extension vocabulary 4

Unit 2 Sounds and basic words 2 6
        Part 1: Core vocabulary 6
        Part 2: Extension vocabulary 8

Unit 3 Sounds and basic words 3 10
        Part 1: Core vocabulary 10
        Part 2: Extension vocabulary 12

Unit 4 The family 14
        Part 1: Core vocabulary 14
        Part 2: Extension vocabulary 17

Unit 5 The world of work 20
        Part 1: Core vocabulary 20
        Part 2: Extension vocabulary 23

Unit 6 Around the house 26
        Part 1: Core vocabulary 26
        Part 2: Extension vocabulary 29

Unit 7 Around town 32
        Part 1: Core vocabulary 32
        Part 2: Extension vocabulary 35

Unit 8   **The world of education** 38
          Part 1: Core vocabulary 38
          Part 2: Extension vocabulary 41

Unit 9   **The Arab World** 44
          Part 1: Core vocabulary 44
          Part 2: Extension vocabulary 47

Unit 10   **Shopping** 50
          Part 1: Core vocabulary 50
          Part 2: Extension vocabulary 53

Unit 11   **Food and drink** 56
          Part 1: Core vocabulary 56
          Part 2: Extension vocabulary 59

Unit 12   **Going out** 62
          Part 1: Core vocabulary 62
          Part 2: Extension vocabulary 65

Unit 13   **Everyday life** 68
          Part 1: Core vocabulary 68
          Part 2: Extension vocabulary 71

Unit 14   **Society and current affairs** 74
          Part 1: Core vocabulary 74
          Part 2: Extension vocabulary 77

Answers to activities 80

 www.bloomsburyonlineresources.com/mastering-arabic-series

Introduction

Mastering Arabic Vocabulary and Pronunciation is a reference and activity book for all beginners and early intermediate students of Arabic.

As a reference book, it provides friendly theme-based vocabulary lists. As an activity book, it helps you to absorb and practise the vocabulary you are learning.

This book assumes you have a reasonable knowledge of the Arabic script and basic grammar.

How to use this book

Each unit of the book is divided into two parts:
- **Part 1**: Core vocabulary, with related activities
- **Part 2**: Extension vocabulary, with related activities.

Part 1 is suitable for early beginners. You can start by working through the core vocabulary and related activities, returning to the extension parts at a later stage.

Part 2 is more suitable for late beginners or early intermediate students. If you are confident of your level, you can complete the core and extension parts together.

The first three units of *Mastering Arabic Vocabulary and Pronunciation* focus on basic vocabulary sets and the pronunciation of individual sounds. Subsequent units focus on a particular theme.

The units have a built-in progression. You should feel you are making progress as you move through the book.

Answers to all the activities are included in the final section of the book. You can also find models for the speaking activities on the audio.

Downloadable audio

Each copy of *Mastering Arabic Vocabulary and Pronunciation* comes with free online audio, available at: www.bloomsburyonlineresources.com/mastering-arabic-series.

All core and extension vocabulary lists are included in the audio, as are listening activities and models for the end-of-section speaking activities. Those parts of the book which are on the audio are marked with this symbol: 🎧. The number under the headphone symbol identifies the audio section online.

Modern Standard Arabic

The vocabulary presented in this book is friendly Modern Standard Arabic which is universally understood in a variety of different situations and will provide you with an excellent base for your written and spoken language.

1 Sounds and basic words 1

Part 1: Core vocabulary

Arabic	Pronunciation	English	Write it yourself
أَنا	anā	I	_____
أَنْتَ	anta	you (masc. sing.)	_____
أَنْتِ	anti	you (fem. sing.)	_____
أَنْتُمْ	antum	you (plural)	_____
هُوَ	huwa	he	_____
هِيَ	hiya	she	_____
نَحْنُ	naḥnu	we	_____
هُمْ	hum	they (masc.)	_____
وَ	wa-	and	_____
هُنا	hunā	here	_____
هُناكَ	hunāka	(over) there	_____
هَلْ ...؟	hal ...?	question word	_____

Pronunciation tip

The letter ح (ḥā')
The letter ح (ḥā') is a breathy 'h' similar to the sound you might make when breathing on glasses to clean them. The letter appears in the list above in the middle of the word for 'we': نَحْنُ (naḥnu). It also appears in names of Arabic origin that might be familiar to you. Listen to these names and repeat the Arabic pronunciation carefully.

أَحْمَد *aḥmad* Ahmed   حَمْدي *ḥamdi* Hamdi

سَحَر *saḥar* Sahar   مُحَمَّد *muḥammad* Mohammed

Activity 1
Match the characters with the speech bubbles, as in the example.

١. نَحْنُ حَمْدي وَمُحَمَّد.
٢. هَلْ أَنْتِ سَحَر؟
٣. أَنا أَحْمَد.
٤. مُحَمَّد هُناكَ.
٥. أَنا سَحَر.
٦. هَلْ أَنْتَ حَمْدي؟

Activity 2
Write the missing Arabic words in the sentences and questions to match the English translation, as in the example.

	English	Arabic
١	I'm Mohammed.	ــــــ أَنا مُحَمَّد.
٢	She's Sahar.	ــــــ سَحَر.
٣	Are you Ahmed?	هَلْ ــــــ أَحْمَد؟
٤	Are you Sahar?	ــــــ ــــــ سَحَر؟
٥	We are here.	ــــــ هُنا.
٦	Are you (plural) here?	هَلْ ــــــ ــــــ ؟
٧	Are they over there?	هَلْ ــــــ ــــــ ؟
٨	I'm Hamdi and he's Ahmed.	ــــــ حَمْدي وَ ــــــ أَحْمَد.

Part 2: Extension vocabulary

Arabic	Pronunciation	English	Write it yourself
أَنْتُما	antumā	you [two] (dual)	_____
أَنْتُنَّ	antunna	you (fem. plural)	_____
هُما	humā	they [two] (dual)	_____
هُنَّ	hunna	they (fem. plural)	_____
أَهْلاً	ahlan	hello	_____
مَرْحَباً	marḥaban	welcome	_____
اِسْمي ...	ismī ...	my name's ...	_____
تَشَرَّفْنا	tasharrafnā	pleased to meet you	_____

> **Language tip**
>
> **The ending ً (-an)**
> Some basic Arabic expressions end with a double *fatḥa* vowel sign (ً)
> pronounced -an. This is often written on top of a silent *alif* (ا). Try to
> remember the spelling and pronunciation of these expressions.
>
> أَهْلاً *ahlan* hello   مَرْحَباً *marḥaban* welcome
> شُكْراً *shukran* thank you   أَيْضاً *aydan* also

Activity 3
Match the Arabic pronouns to their English equivalents, as in the example.

a she
b they (fem.)
c you (masc. sing.)
d we
e they (masc.)
f they (dual)

g you (fem. pl.)
h you (fem. sing.)
i I
j you (masc. pl.)
k he
l you (dual)

١ نَحْنُ _d_
٢ هُوَ __
٣ أنا __
٤ هُنَّ __
٥ أَنْتِ __
٦ أَنْتُما __
٧ أَنْتُنَّ __
٨ أَنْتَ __
٩ هُمْ __
١٠ هُما __
١١ هِيَ __
١٢ أَنْتُمْ __

Sounds and basic words 1

Activity 4

Listen to your audio track. The coach, Captain Mahmoud, is trying to organise his new group of young men and women into teams. Listen and try to decide if the Arabic statements below are true (T) or false (F).

كابِتِن مَحْمود: هَلْ أَنْتَ حامِد؟ هَل أَنْتَ سامِح؟

حامِد: أَنا حامِد! سامِح هُناكَ!

كابِتِن مَحْمود: أَهْلاً حامِد. هَلْ أَنْتِ سَحَر؟

سَميحة: أَنا سَميحة. أَنا اِسْمي سَميحة. وهِيَ سَحَر.

كابِتِن مَحْمود: أَهْلاً سَميحة! مَرْحَباً سَحَر! تَشَرَّفْنا!

سَميحة: شُكْراً، كابِتِن مَحْمود!

حامِد: نَحْنُ أَيْضاً تَشَرَّفْنا!

١ سامِح هُناكَ. ☐

٢ حامِد هُناكَ. ☐

٣ سَميحة وسَحَر هُنا. ☐

٤ سَميحة وسَحَر هُناكَ. ☐

٥ الكابِتِن اِسْمُهُ أَحْمَد. ☐

٦ الكابِتِن اِسْمُهُ مَحْمود. ☐

Language tip

Short vowels

Throughout the first units, we include the short vowel marks – *fatḥa (a), ḍamma (u)* and *kasra (i)*. In subsequent units, we still include the short vowels in the core and extension vocabulary lists, since this is useful for pronunciation. However, we also start to encourage you to recognise words in context without these short vowels, as this is how they will generally appear in Arabic text for native speakers. When writing Arabic yourself, you can include the short vowels or not as you prefer.

2 Sounds and basic words 2

Part 1: Core vocabulary

5

Arabic	Pronunciation	English	Write it yourself
هَذا	hādhā	this (masc.)	_____
هَذِهِ	hādhihi	this (fem.)	_____
أَيْنَ؟	ayna?	where?	_____
ما؟	mā?	what?	_____
مَنْ؟	man?	who?	_____
كَبير	kabīr	big/large	_____
صَغير	ṣaghīr	small	_____
جَديد	jadīd	new	_____
قَديم	qadīm	old	_____
مَكْسور	maksūr	broken	_____
سَليم	salīm	unbroken	_____
طَويل	ṭawīl	tall/long	_____
قَصير	qaṣīr	short	_____

Activity 1
Write هَذا or هَذِهِ in the gaps, as in the example.

١ هَذا بَيْت.
٢ _____ دَرّاجة.
٣ _____ باب.
٤ _____ مِفْتاح.
٥ _____ حَقيبة.
٦ _____ قَلَم.
٧ _____ سَيّارة.
٨ _____ خَيْمة.

Sounds and basic words 2

Pronunciation tip

The emphatic letters
There are four emphatic Arabic letters: ص (ṣād), ض (ḍād), ط (ṭā') and ظ (ẓā'). These letters are pronounced towards the back of the mouth. The sounds differ from their non-emphatic equivalents in much the same way as the initial sounds of the English 'Tim' and 'Tom', or 'silly' and 'sorry', differ. Listen carefully to these pairs of Arabic names. The first name starts with a non-emphatic sound and the second with its emphatic equivalent. Repeat the Arabic pronunciation.

سَميرة samīra Samira   تَميم tamīm Tamim

صَباح ṣabāḥ Sabah   طاهِر ṭāhir Tahir

دينا dīnā Dina   زَيْد zayd Zayd

ضُحَى ḍuḥā Duha   ظافِر ẓāfir Zafir

Activity 2
Sabah is talking to her brother Zayd about the website of a cycling club that she has joined in order to keep fit. Listen and put the transcript of the conversation in the correct order, as in the example.

Additional vocabulary
heroine بَطَلة   woman سَيِّدة   all of them كُلُّها

☐ **زيد:** بَطَلة كَبيرة؟ ما اِسْمُها؟

☐ **صَباح:** هَذِهِ بَطَلة كَبيرة في الدَّرّاجات.

☒ **زيد:** ما هَذِهِ يا صَباح؟

☐ **صَباح:** اِسْمُها «كابتِن دينا أَحْمَد».

☐ **زيد:** ومَنْ هَذِهِ السَّيِّدة الطَّويلة؟

☐ **صَباح:** هَذِهِ هِيَ الدَّرّاجات الجَديدة. الدَّرّاجات القَديمة كُلُّها صَغيرة ومَكْسورة.

Part 2: Extension vocabulary

Arabic	Pronunciation	English	Write it yourself
ذَلِكَ	dhālika	that (masc.)	_____
تِلْكَ	tilka	that (fem.)	_____
كَيْفَ؟	kayfa?	how?	_____
ثَقيل	thaqīl	heavy	_____
خَفيف	khafīf	light	_____
سَريع	sarīᴄ	fast	_____
جَميل	jamīl	beautiful	_____

Pronunciation tip

Dagger alif
A few Arabic words are written with a *fatha* pronounced as a long *ā* rather than as a short *a*. Three of these words are in the Unit 2 vocabulary lists: هَذا *hādhā* ('this' masc.), هَذِهِ *hādhihi* ('this' fem.) and ذَلِكَ *dhālika*, ('that' masc.). Another common example is the word for 'but': لَكِن *lākin*. Pay special attention to the pronunciation of these words.

The traditional spelling is to add a small *alif* mark above the letter (e.g., هَٰذا). This mark is known as a 'dagger *alif*' due to its shape. But in general a regular *fatha* is used in modern Arabic. The most notable exception is in the spelling of the Arabic word for 'God': الله *allāh*.

Activity 3
Write the missing Arabic question words to match the English translation, as in the example. Then cover the Arabic and try to write out the complete questions using the English prompts only.

What's this?	١ ___ما___ هَذا؟	
Where's the key?	٢ _____ المِفْتاح؟	
How are you? ['how's the state?']	٣ _____ الحال؟	
Who are they?	٤ _____ هُمْ؟	
Is the bag heavy?	٥ _____ الحَقيبة ثَقيلة؟	
What's the girl's name?	٦ _____ اِسْم البِنْت؟	

Activity 4

Listen to Sabah describing her new racing bicycle, which she has named 'The Feather' (الريشة *ar-rīsha*). First read what she says below, and the additional vocabulary, and decide what type of word might be missing from the gap. Then listen and write in the missing words you hear on your audio track, as in the example.

Additional vocabulary

because لِأَنَّ   like مِثْل   story قِصّة

هذه ـــــــ هِيَ دَرّاجَتي الجَديدة.

اِسْمُها "الريشة". ـــــــ لِأَنَّ دَرّاجَتي

سَريعة وَ ـــــــ وَ ـــــــ مِثْل الريشة!

هِيَ ـــــــ قِصّة ـــــــ دَرّاجَتي!

🛈 Language tip

Grammatical features of Arabic

Throughout this guide, we are assuming a knowledge of the basic grammatical features of Arabic. These include the feminine ending ة (*-a*), for example دَرّاجة قَديمة *darrāja qadīma* ('an old bicycle'); the possessive endings, for example دَرّاجَتي *darrājatī* ('my bicycle'), and the conjugation of verbs, for example أَشْرَب، يَشْرَب *ashrab, yashrab* ('I drink, he drinks'). You should refer to an Arabic course, for example *Mastering Arabic 1*, and/or a grammar guide, for example *Mastering Arabic Grammar* (published in the U.S. as *Easy Arabic Grammar*) to use alongside this guide.

3 Sounds and basic words 3

Part 1: Core vocabulary

Arabic	Pronunciation	English	Write it yourself
في	fī	in	_____
عَلَى	𐤏ala	on	_____
تَحْتَ	taḥta	under	_____
فَوْقَ	fawqa	above	_____
بَيْنَ	bayna	between	_____
عِنْدَ	𐤏inda	at/'have'	_____
مِنْ	min	from	_____
سَكَنَ/يَسْكُنْ	sakana/yaskun	to live	_____
دَرَسَ/يَدْرُس	darasa/yadrus	to study	_____
ذَهَبَ/يَذْهَب	dhahaba/yadh-hab	to go	_____
كَتَبَ/يَكْتُبْ	kataba/yaktub	to write	_____
جَلَسَ/يَجْلِس	jalasa/yajlis	to sit	_____

Pronunciation tip

The letter ع (𐤏ayn)
The guttural sound of the letter ع (𐤏ayn) is particular to Arabic. The letter ع appears in the list above as the initial sound of the word 'at/have', عِنْدَ (𐤏inda), and 'on', عَلَى (𐤏ala). It also appears as the initial sound of the word 'Arab' itself, عَرَب (𐤏arab), as well as in the middle of the word for 'yes': نَعَمْ (na𐤏am). Some Arab nationalities also contain this sound. Listen and repeat the Arabic pronunciation carefully.

عِراقيّ 𐤏irāqī Iraqi   عُمانيّ 𐤏umānī Omani   سَعودي sa𐤏ūdī Saudi

Sounds and basic words 3

Activity 1
Match the speech bubbles to the picture clues, as in the example.

Language tip

الـ (al-)

There are a few key points to note when you use الـ *al-* ('the'):

- الـ *al-* is written connected to the front of the word that follows: البَيْت *al-bayt* 'the house'.

- The Arabic alphabet is divided into *sun letters* and *moon letters*. Initial sun letters 'take over' the *l* sound of الـ *al-*. This can be shown with a *shadda* sign (ّ) over the initial letter, for example: الدَّرَّاجة *ad-darrāja* 'the bicycle'; السَّمَكة *as-samaka* 'the fish'.

- الـ *al-* will drop the *a* sound if the word before ends with a vowel, for example: في البَيْت *fī l-bayt* 'in the house'. *This only affects the pronunciation and not the spelling.*

Part 2: Extension vocabulary

Arabic	Pronunciation	English	Write it yourself
بَعْدَ	baɛda	after	_____
قَبْلَ	qabla	before	_____
مَعَ	maɛa	with	_____
إلى	ila	to/towards	_____
عَرَفَ/يَعْرِف	ɛarafa/yaɛrif	to know	_____
سَمِعَ/يَسْمَع	samiɛa/yasmaɛ	to hear	_____
قالَ/يَقول	qāla/yaqūl	to say	_____
فَعَلَ/يَفْعَل	faɛala/yafɛal	to do	_____
رَجَعَ/يَرْجِع	rajaɛa/yarjiɛ	to return	_____

Activity 2

Match the Arabic verbs to their English equivalents, for example 1b. Then cover the Arabic and try to write out the verbs using the English prompts only.

a I know

b we say

c you hear *(masc. sing.)*

d he goes

e we live

f you do *(fem. sing.)*

g I study

h she returns

i we sit

j I write

١ نَقول

٢ تَرْجِع

٣ تَفْعَلين

٤ أَعْرِف

٥ نَجْلِس

٦ تَسْمَع

٧ أَكْتُب

٨ يَذْهَب

٩ نَسْكُن

١٠ أَدْرُس

Sounds and basic words 3

>
> **Pronunciation tip**
>
> **Special ending** (*alif maqṣūra*)
> A few Arabic words have an ending written with the final shape of the letter *yā'* without the two dots below: ى . This ending is called *alif maqṣūra* ('shortened *alif*') and is pronounced *a*. Two words in the lists opposite have this ending: عَلَى ʿala ('on') and إلى ʿila ('to/towards').
> *Alif maqṣūra* is also a common ending for feminine Arabic names:
>
> مُنَى *muna* Mona   سَلْمَى *salma* Salma
> لَيْلَى *layla* Leila   هُدَى *huda* Hoda

Activity 3
Listen to Salem and Hoda having a chat as they walk in the park and read the transcript below. Then find the Arabic phrases, as in the example.

Additional vocabulary

bridge جِسْر   office مَكْتَب   university جامِعة

هُدَى: أنا أَذْهَب إلى الجامِعة بالمِتْرو لِأَنَّني أَسْكُن هُناكَ، بَعْدَ الجِسْر.

سالِم: وَماذا تَفْعَلين وَأَنْتِ في المِتْرو؟

هُدَى: أَجْلِس بِجانِب الشُّبّاك، وأَدْرُس الفَرَنْسيّة على الهاتِف. وَأَنْتَ، أَيْنَ تَسْكُن؟

سالِم: نَحْنُ نَسْكُن فَوْقَ مَكْتَب، قَريب مِن الجامِعة.

هُدَى: وَهَل تَذْهَب إلى الجامِعة بالدَّرّاجة؟

سالِم: نَعَمْ، أَذْهَب وَأَرْجِع بِدَرّاجَتي السَّريعة!

near the university ٧	next to the window ٤	to the university ١
		إلى الجامِعة
by bike ٨	on the phone ٥	by metro ٢
on my fast bike ٩	above an office ٦	after the bridge ٣

The family

Part 1: Core vocabulary

14

Arabic	Pronunciation	English	Write it yourself
عائِلة (ات)	ɛā'ila (āt)	family [general]	_____
أُسْرة (أُسَر)	usra (usar)	family [immediate]	_____
أُمّ (أُمَّهات)	umm (ummahāt)	mother	_____
أب (آباء)	ab (ābā')	father	_____
زَوْج (أَزْواج)	zawj (azwāj)	husband	_____
زَوْجة (ات)	zawja (āt)	wife	_____
جَدّ (أَجْداد)	jadd (ajdād)	grandfather	_____
جَدّة (ات)	jadda (āt)	grandmother	_____
أَخ (إِخْوة)	akh (ikhwa)	brother	_____
أُخْت (أَخَوات)	ukht (akhawāt)	sister	_____
اِبْن (أَبْناء)	ibn (abnā')	son	_____
اِبْنة (بَنات)	ibna (banāt)	daughter	_____
طِفْل (أَطْفال)	ṭifl (aṭfāl)	child	_____
مُتَزَوِّج (ون)	mutazawwij (ūn)	married	_____

❗ Language tip

Words in the main units (4 to 14) are presented with their plurals in brackets: either ات āt /ون ūn, or broken plurals spelt out individually. You can hear the singular and plural words on the downloadable audio.

Regular adjectives are shown in the masculine singular; add the ending ة (-a) to refer to a female. Other irregular patterns are given separately.

The family

> **Pronunciation tip**
>
> **The letter خ** (*khā'*)
> The letter خ (*khā'*) is the sound you might make when clearing your throat, similar to the Scottish pronunciation of the sound 'ch' in 'loch'. The letter appears in the Arabic words for 'brother', أخ (*akh*), and 'sister', أُخْت (*ukht*). It is also the first letter of these Arabic names that might be familiar to you. Listen to the names and repeat the Arabic pronunciation carefully.
>
> خالِد *khālid* Khalid   خُلود *khulūd* Khulud
>
> خَليل *khalīl* Khalil   خَديجة *khadīja* Khadija

Activity 1
Pair the male and female family-related words, for example 1d.

أُخْت	e	اِبْنة	a	أب	5	زَوْج	1
مُتَزَوِّجة	f	أُمّ	b	طِفْل	6	جَدّ	2
جَدّة	g	طِفْلة	c	مُتَزَوِّج	7	اِبْن	3
		زَوْجة	d			أخ	4

Activity 2
Imagine you are introducing yourself and some of your family, for example:

أَهْلاً. أنا اِسْمي ...   Hello. My name's ...

هَذا أبي ...   This is my father, ...

وَهَذِهِ أُخْتي ...   And this is my sister, ...

Introduce yourself, and at least two female relatives and two male relatives by name. Practise the introductions out loud. You can listen to the model and then record yourself, getting some feedback from an Arabic speaker if you can. When you are confident, write down your introductions.

_____

_____

_____

_____

Activity 3

Who is who? Khuloud is talking about her family. Read what she says and write the names of her relatives under their pictures on the family tree.

Additional vocabulary　twins　تَوْأَمان

اسمي خُلود وأنا مُتَزَوِّجة.
زَوْجي اسمُهُ توم، وهو أَمْريكيّ.
أَبي، صالِح، مِن بَيْروت وأمّي، خَديجة، مِن عُمان.
عِنْدَنا أَرْبَعة أَطْفال: ثَلاثة أَبْناء: خالِد، والتَّوْأَمان سامي ويوسُف؛ وابنة واحِدة اسمُها نورة.

خُلود

Language tip

Short vowels
High-frequency words and common vocabulary connected to the theme of a unit will sometimes appear within reading activities without short vowels. This is to encourage you to recognise words without the short vowels as this is how they will generally appear in Arabic text for native speakers.

Part 2: Extension vocabulary

Arabic	Pronunciation	English	Write it yourself
عَمّ (أَعْمام)	ɛamm (aɛmām)	paternal uncle	_____
عَمّة (ات)	ɛamma (āt)	paternal aunt	_____
خال (أَخْوال)	khāl (akhwāl)	maternal uncle	_____
خالة (ات)	khāla (āt)	maternal aunt	_____
حَم (أَحْماء)	ḥam (aḥmā')	father-in-law	_____
حَماة (حَمَوات)	ḥamāh (ḥamawāt)	mother-in-law	_____
حَفيد (أَحْفاد)	ḥafīd (aḥfād)	grandson	_____
حَفيدة (ات)	ḥafīda (āt)	granddaughter	_____
خَطيب (خُطَباء)	khaṭīb (khuṭabā')	fiancé	_____
خَطيبة (ات)	khaṭība (āt)	fiancée	_____
والِدايَ	wālidāya	my parents	_____
أَعْزَب/عَزْباء	aɛzab/ɛazbā'	single [masc./fem.]	_____
مَخْطوب (ون)	makhṭūb (ūn)	engaged	_____
مُطَلَّق (ون)	muṭallaq (ūn)	divorced	_____
وُلِدَ/يولَد	wulida/yūlad	to be born	_____
تَزَوَّجَ/يَتَزَوَّج	tazawwaja/ yatazawwaj	to get married	_____

> **Language tip**
>
> **Masculine plural ending**
> The masculine plural ending ون ūn can sometimes be written and pronounced as ين īn. This depends on how the plural is used in a sentence.
>
> كُلُّهُمْ مُتَزَوِّجون. kulluhum mutazawwijūn They are all married.
>
> حَياة المُطَلَّقين صَعْبة. ḥayāt al-muṭallaqīn ṣaɛba.
> The life of divorced people is hard.

Activity 4
Identify the relatives from the description, for example ١c.

١ أُخت أبي هي...
a خالَتي   b حَفيدَتي   c عَمَّتي

٤ أُمّ أبي هي...
a عَمَّتي   b حَفيدَتي   c جَدَّتي

٢ أبو زوجَتي هو...
a عمّي   b حَمي   c حَماتي

٥ أخو أُمّي هو...
a خالي   b عَمّي   c حَمي

٣ ابن ابنَتي هو...
a حَفيدي   b جَدّي   c أبي

٦ أُمّ زوجي هي...
a حَماتي   b حَفيدَتي   c جَدَّتي

Activity 5
Complete the English sentences to match the Arabic, as in the example.

١ يَسكُن والدِايَ مَعَ جَدَّتي.
My _parents_ live with my _____.

٢ قالَ جدّي إنَّهُ يَذهَب إلى الحَديقة مَعَ أحفادِه كُلّ يَوْم.
My _____ said that he goes to the park with his _____ every day.

٣ يَعمَل أبناء عَمَّتي مَعاً في مَصنَع السَّجّاد.
My _____ work together _____ a carpet factory.

٤ أنا وخَطيبَتي سَنَزور أُسرَتَها في قَرية "قَصر النَّخيل".
My _____ and I will visit her _____ in the village of 'Palace of Palms'.

٥ حَياة عَمَّتي صَعْبة لِأنَّها مُطَلَّقة وأطفالُها صِغار.
The life of my _____ is hard because she is _____ and her _____ are young.

٦ دَفَعَ خالي كُلّ تَكاليف فَرَح أختي الكبيرة.
My _____ paid all the expenses of the wedding of my older _____.

> **! Language tip**
>
> To talk about cousins, nephews, nieces, sisters-in-law or brothers-in-law, you need to be specific about their relationship to you, for example:
>
> اِبن عَمَّتي *ibn ɛammatī* the son of my paternal aunt
>
> اِبنة خالي *ibnat khālī* the daughter of my maternal uncle
>
> أُخت زَوْجي *ukht zawjī* the sister of my husband
>
> اِبنة أخي *ibnat akhī* the daughter of my brother

The family

Activity 6
Ahmad is talking about his family. Read what he says and try to decide if the sentences below are true (T) or false (F). Concentrate on getting the gist of the passage, rather than about understanding every word.

أنا اسمي أحمَد، وزوجتي اسمُها خديجة. ابنتي الكبيرة اسمُها سامية، وعُمرُها سبع سَنَوات. إسماعيل عُمرُه أربع سَنَوات، وأميرة عُمرُها ستَّة شُهور فَقَط.

وُلِدتُ هنا، في بَيت أبي الكبير، بِجانِب البَحر. ولَكِنَّني الآن أسكُن في شَقَّة كَبيرة قَريبة من مَدرَسة أطفالي. أيّام الجُمعة، نزور والِدَيَّ ونأكُل الغَداء مَعاً. كُلّ عائلتي تُحِبّ البَحر.

هذه صورة خديجة مع ابنة عمِّها، شَريفة، وخطيبها خالد، في الأسبوع الماضي.

١ أحمد مُتَزَوِّج. ☐
٢ أحمد عِندَه أربعة أطفال. ☐
٣ أسماء أطفاله هي سامية وإسماعيل وأميرة. ☐
٤ أميرة عُمرُها ستّ سَنَوات. ☐
٥ يَسكُن أحمد الآن مَعَ أبيه وأمّه في البيت الكبير. ☐
٦ لا تُحِبّ عائلة أحمد البَحر. ☐
٧ تَزور الأُسرة والِدَيْ أحمد أيّام الجُمعة. ☐
٨ ابنة عم خديجة مَخطوبة. ☐

Activity 7
Now talk about your own family situation. Use the prompts below and the passage above to help you, adjusting to the feminine if you are female. Write down notes for your description first, and then record yourself. You can listen to the model to review your pronunciation. You can also write up your description using your notes. Show your work to an Arabic speaker if you can.

My name's ...   ... أنا اِسمي
I'm married/single/engaged/divorced   أنا مُتَزَوِّج/أعزَب/مَخطوب/مُطَلَّق
I have ... children/sons/sisters, etc.   عِندي ... أطفال/أبناء/أخَوات، ألخ
I was born in ...   ... وُلِدتُ في
but now I live in ... with my ...   ولكِنِّي الآن أسكُن في ... مَعَ ...ـي
On Fridays/Saturdays/Sundays, we visit my ...   أيّام الجُمعة/السَّبت/الأحَد نَزور ...ـي

5 The world of work

Part 1: Core vocabulary

19

Arabic	Pronunciation	English	Write it yourself
مُدَرِّس (ون)	mudarris (ūn)	teacher	_____
مُحاسِب (ون)	muḥāsib (ūn)	accountant	_____
خَبّاز (ون)	khabbāz (ūn)	baker	_____
مُمَرِّض (ون)	mumarriḍ (ūn)	nurse	_____
مُهَنْدِس (ون)	muhandis (ūn)	engineer	_____
نَجّار (ون)	najjār (ūn)	carpenter	_____
طَبّاخ (ون)	ṭabbākh (ūn)	cook	_____
مُصَوِّر (ون)	muṣawwir (ūn)	photographer	_____
طَبيب (أَطِبّاء)	ṭabīb (aṭibbā')	doctor	_____
مُدير (ون)	mudīr (ūn)	manager	_____
مُساعِد (ون)	musāʿid (ūn)	assistant	_____
مُوَظَّف (ون)	muwaẓẓaf (ūn)	employee	_____
عامِل (عُمّال)	ʿāmil (ʿummāl)	labourer	_____
فَنّان (ون)	fannān (ūn)	artist	_____
عَمَل (أَعْمال)	ʿamal (aʿmāl)	work	_____
عَمِلَ/يَعْمَل	ʿamila/yaʿmal	to work	_____
مَكْتَب (مَكاتِب)	maktab (makātib)	office	_____
مَصْنَع (مَصانِع)	maṣnaʿ (maṣāniʿ)	factory	_____
مُسْتَشْفَى (مُسْتَشْفَيات)	mustashfa (mustashfayāt)	hospital	_____

The world of work

> **Pronunciation tip**
>
> **Pronouncing double letters** (*shadda*)
> Many Arabic words for professions contain a double letter sound, for example 'artist' فَنَّان (*fannān*), and 'photographer', مُصَوِّر (*muṣawwir*).
> In written Arabic, the double sound is indicated by a small 'w' sign above the letter called a شَدَّة (*shadda*), or 'emphasis', a word which itself appropriately includes the doubling sign. In English, a double letter changes the sound <u>before</u>, for example 'bitter' and 'biter'. However, in Arabic the letter itself needs to be doubled or 'emphasised'. Listen again to the vocabulary list and copy the pronunciation of the *shadda* carefully.

Activity 1
Guess my profession from the equipment I left behind in your apartment, and then write the profession below.

Activity 2
A friend appears always to have issues. Choose the right person to help him.

He wants to mend his cupboard. ٤

a نَجَّار b خَبَّاز c مُدير

He has chest pains. ١

a خَبَّاز b طَبيب c مُهَنْدِس

He would like a portrait of his dog. ٥

a طَبَّاخ b فَنَّان c طَبيب

He needs a passport photo. ٢

a مُمَرِّضة b طَبَّاخ c مُصَوِّر

He has problems with his tax return. ٦

a طَبيب b مُحاسِب c مُصَوِّر

He wants to learn Chinese. ٣

a مُدَرِّس b نَجَّار c مُحاسِب

Activity 3

🎧 20

Listen to a female broadcaster (مُذيعة *mudhīʿa*) interviewing Mohammed, the chief engineer (كَبير المُهَندِسين *kabīr al-muhandisīn*). Choose a profession from the list on page 20 to fill the gaps, as in the example. (The professions can be plural so listen carefully.) Then answer the questions below in English.

المُذيعة: هل أنتَ ___مُدير___ هذا المَصنَع الجديد؟

مُحَمَّد: لا. أنا _____ المُدير، وكبير الـ_____ .

المُذيعة: كَم عَدَد الـ_____ والـ_____ هنا؟

مُحَمَّد: نحن ألف.

المُذيعة: وما هي ساعات العَمَل هنا؟

مُحَمَّد: نَعمَل ٢٤ ساعة كلّ يوم. بَعضَ الـ_____ يَسكُنون هناك، وَراء المَصنَع.

المُذيعة: هل أنتَ تَسكُن مَعَهُم، هناك، وَراء المَصنَع؟

مُحَمَّد: لا. أنا أسكُن في قَصر صَغير بِجانِب البَحر.

1. What are Mohammed's two roles in the factory?
2. How many people work in the factory altogether?
3. What hours does the factory operate?
4. Where do some of the factory employees and workers live?
5. Where does Mohammed live?
6. Do you think the factory is near the coast? Why do you think this?

Activity 4

🎧 21

Now say something about your own occupation, real or imaginary. Include what you do, where you work and what your hours are. Practise out loud, listening to the model for help with pronunciation. Then write down your passage.

_____

_____

_____

The world of work

Part 2: Extension vocabulary

Arabic	Pronunciation	English	Write it yourself
مَندوب (ون)	mandūb (ūn)	representative	_____
بَنّاء (ون)	bannā' (ūn)	builder	_____
مُصَمِّم (ون)	muṣammim (ūn)	designer	_____
مُحامٍ (مُحامون)	muḥāmin (muḥāmūn)	lawyer	_____
سائِق (ون)	sā'iq (ūn)	driver	_____
صُحُفيّ (ون)	ṣuḥufiy (ūn)	journalist	_____
شَرِكة (ات)	sharika (āt)	company	_____
وَظيفة (وَظائِف)	waẓīfa (waẓā'if)	job	_____
راتِب (رَواتِب)	rātib (rawātib)	salary	_____
مِهْنة (مِهَن)	mihna (mihan)	profession	_____
اِجْتِماع (ات)	ijtimāɛ (āt)	meeting	_____
مَبيعات	mabīɛāt	sales	_____
مَحَلّ (ات)	maḥall (āt)	store	_____
أدارَ/يُدير	adāra/yudīr	to manage	_____
ساعَدَ/يُساعِد	sāɛada/yusāɛid	to assist	_____
صَنَعَ/يَصْنَع	ṣanaɛa/yaṣnaɛ	to manufacture	_____

> **Language tip**
>
> **Arabic roots**
> Recognising the three root sounds present in most Arabic words will help you to link related meanings formed from the same root. For example, عامل (ɛāmil), 'worker'/'labourer', and أعْمَل (aɛmal), 'I work', from the root ع/م/ل (ɛ/m/l), 'working'; or شَرِكة (sharika), 'company', and شَريك (sharīk), 'partner', from the root ش/ر/ك (sh/r/k), 'sharing'. Mastering the roots and their patterns takes time but gradually you will be able to use them to expand your vocabulary organically.

Activity 5
Ismail is talking about his family's revenue streams. Read what he says, and then decide which of the following sentences are true (T) and which are false (F). (Pay special attention to sentence six because it can be tricky!)

> أنا إسماعيل أمين. أعمَل في شَرِكة كبيرة وقَوِيّة، ولكنّ الرَّواتِب فيها صغيرة وضعيفة. أنا أعمَل في الشَّرِكة في الصباح، وبَعدَ الظُّهر أعمَل كَسائِق تاكسي. أبي، حَسَن أمين، عِندَهُ تاكسي. يَعمَل هو على التاكسي في الصباح، وبَعدَ الظُّهر يُعطيني المِفتاح. تعمَل زَوْجَتي بَهيجة، وأُختُها شادية، في مَحَلّ حَماتي لِبَيْع الحَقائِب. رَواتِب المَحَلّ ضعيفة أيضاً، ولكنّها تُساعِدنا.

١ يَعمَل إسماعيل كَسائِق تاكسي بَعدَ الظُّهر. ☐
٢ أبو إسماعيل اسمُه أمين حَسَن. ☐
٣ يَعمَل حَسَن كَسائِق تاكسي في الصباح. ☐
٤ شادية هي أُخت إسماعيل. ☐
٥ رَواتِب مَحَلّ الحَقائِب ضعيفة. ☐
٦ تَعمَل بَهيجة في مَحَلّ أُمِّها. ☐

Activity 6
From what Ismail says, match the Arabic words and expressions below to their English equivalents. Can you say the words correctly without the vowels?

a	company	f	she works	٦ قويّة	١	يعمل
b	store	g	strong	٧ رواتب	٢	ضعيفة
c	for selling	h	driver	٨ تعمل	٣	سائق
d	weak/low	i	salaries	٩ محلّ	٤	أعمل
e	I work	j	he works	١٠ لبيع	٥	شركة

Activity 7

Listen to my plans for tomorrow, and fill in the blanks in my calendar.

Activity 8

Now talk about your own family and what they do. Use the prompts below and the vocabulary in this unit to help you. Remember to use the feminine in brackets if appropriate. Write down notes and then record yourself. Play the model to review your pronunciation. You can also write up your description using your notes. Show your work to an Arabic speaker if you can.

...ـي هو (هي) ... is a ... My

يَعمَل (تَعمَل) في ... ... He/she ... works in

...ـي هو (هي) مُدير(ة)/مُساعِد(ة)/مُوَظَّف(ة) في ... كبير(ة)/صغير(ة)
My ... is a manager/an assistant/an employee in a large/small ...

...ـي يُدير (تُدير) مَصنَعاً يَصنَع .../مَحَلًّا لِبيع ...
My ... manages a factory which manufactures ... /a store for selling ...

6 Around the house

Part 1: Core vocabulary

25

Arabic	Pronunciation	English	Write it yourself
غُرْفة (غُرَف)	ghurfa (ghuraf)	room	_____
شَقّة (شُقَق)	shaqqa (shuqaq)	apartment	_____
مائِدة (مَوائِد)	mā'ida (mawā'id)	table	_____
كُرْسيّ (كَراسي)	kursīy (karāsī)	chair	_____
سَرير (أَسِرّة)	sarīr (assirra)	bed	_____
ثَلّاجة (ات)	thallāja (āt)	fridge	_____
فُرْن (أَفْران)	furn (afrān)	oven	_____
خِزانة (ات)	khizāna (āt)	cupboard	_____
أَريكة (أَرائِك)	arīka (arā'ik)	sofa	_____
سَجّادة (سَجّاد)	sajjāda/sajjād	carpet	_____
وِسادة (وَسائِد)	wisāda (wasā'id)	pillow/cushion	_____
باب (أَبْواب)	bāb (abwāb)	door	_____
شُبّاك (شَبابيك)	shubbāk (shabābīk)	window	_____
مَطْبَخ (مَطابِخ)	maṭbakh (maṭābikh)	kitchen	_____
حَمّام (ات)	ḥammām (āt)	bathroom	_____
غُرْفة نَوْم (غُرَف نَوْم)	ghurfat nawm (ghuraf nawm)	bedroom	_____
حَديقة (حَدائِق)	ḥadīqa (ḥadā'iq)	garden	_____
(لَيْسَ) هُناكَ ...	(laysa) hunāka ...	there is (not)/are (not)	_____

Around the house

Pronunciation tip

The letter غ (ghayn)
The sound represented by the letter غ (ghayn) is pronounced at the back of the throat as if gargling, similar to the French pronunciation of 'rue'. It is the first letter of the Arabic word for 'room', غُرْفة (ghurfa), and the middle letter of the word for 'small', صَغير (ṣaghīr). It is also the first letter of these Arabic names. Listen and repeat the pronunciation carefully.

غالِب ghālib Ghalib   غادة ghāda Ghada

غَيْث ghayth Ghaith   غالِية ghāliya Ghalya

Activity 1
In Arabic, write the name of the object each man is carrying.

Activity 2
Match the phrases with their opposites, for example ١e.

a الخِزانة الصغيرة	١	على السرير
b لَيْسَ هناك وَسائد	٢	بِجانِب باب الحَمّام
c الثلّاجة هناك	٣	أمام الشبّاك
d بَعيد عَن باب الحَمّام	٤	الخِزانة الكبيرة
e تَحتَ السرير	٥	الثلّاجة هنا
f وَراء الشبّاك	٦	هناك وَسائد

Activity 3

Geraldine McMurphy is moving house in Cairo, but she doesn't speak Arabic. She's given you these instructions about where she wants her furniture. Write them out in Arabic for the removal men. The first instruction has been started for you.

1 the small bed in the small room

السرير الصغير في _____

2 the big cupboard beside the sofa

_____

3 the fridge beside kitchen door ('door of the kitchen')

_____

4 the big bed and the chairs in the bedroom

_____

5 all the pillows on the big bed

_____

6 the oven between the window and the door

_____

Activity 4

Give a basic description of your home. Use these prompts to help you:

أَسكُن في بَيْت كبير/شَقّة صغيرة I live in a large house/a small apartment

هناك غُرفَتان/ثَلاث غُرَف، إلخ There are two rooms/three rooms, etc.

في غُرفَتي/في المَطبَخ هناك ... In my room/in the kitchen, there is/are ...

ولكن لَيْسَ هناك ... But there isn't/aren't ...

Practise out loud, listening to the model for help with pronunciation. You can record yourself if you want to review yourself, and get some feedback from an Arabic speaker. When you are confident, write down your description.

_____

_____

_____

Around the house

Part 2: Extension vocabulary

Arabic	Pronunciation	English	Write it yourself
شُرْفة (ات)	shurfa (āt)	balcony	_____
غُرْفة مَعيشة (غُرَف مَعيشة)	ghurfat maɛīsha (ghuraf maɛīsha)	living room	_____
حَمّام سِباحة (حَمّامات سِباحة)	ḥammām sibāḥa (ḥammāmāt sibāḥa)	swimming pool	_____
سَقْف (أَسْقُف)	saqf (asquf)	ceiling	_____
سَطْح (أَسْطُح)	saṭḥ (asṭuḥ)	roof	_____
سُلَّم (سَلالِم)	sullam (salālim)	stairs	_____
مِصْعَد (مَصاعِد)	miṣɛad (maṣāɛid)	elevator	_____
طابِق (طَوابِق)	ṭābiq (ṭawābiq)	storey/floor	_____
سِتار (سَتائِر)	sitār/satā'ir	curtain	_____
مُكَيِّف الهَواء	mukayyif al-hawā'	air conditioner	_____
غَسّالة (ات)	ghassāla (āt)	washing machine	_____
سُفْرة (ات)	sufra (āt)	dining table	_____
حَديث	ḥadīth	modern	_____
تَقْليديّ	taqlīdī	traditional	_____
فاخِر	fākhir	luxurious	_____
مُريح	murīḥ	comfortable	_____
واسِع	wāsiɛ	spacious	_____
مَفْروش	mafrūsh	furnished	_____
تَكَوَّنَ/يَتَكَوَّن مِن	takawwana/yatakawwan min	to consist of	_____
اِسْتَأْجَرَ/يَسْتَأْجِر	ista'jara/yasta'jir	to rent	_____

Activity 5

Match the positions in the box to the picture clues, for example ١f.

٦ على السلّم	٤ أمام المصعد	١ فوق الغسّالة
٧ وراء الستار	٥ بجانب حمّام السباحة	٢ في المطبخ
		٣ تحت السجّادة

Activity 6

Ghalib is describing his life on the road. Read what he says, and then decide which of the sentences on page 31 is true (T) and which is false (F).

أنا اسمي غالب. أنا مَندوب مَبيعات في المَمْلَكة العَرَبيّة السَّعوديّة. أَنْتَقِل من مدينة إلى مدينة، ومن فُندُق إلى فُندُق. أمس، كُنتُ في الرِّياض. كانَتْ غُرفَتي في الفُندُق الفاخِر هناك مِثل غُرفَتي هنا، اليوم. ولكنَّني اليوم في الدَّمام. غَداً، سَأطير إلى أبها، وسَتَكون غُرفَتي في الفُندُق هناك مِثل غُرفَتي اليوم، وغُرفة الأمس. سَتَكون هناك كَراسي مُريحة، ومائدة كبيرة وثلّاجة صغيرة. مُكَيِّف الهَواء سَيَكون فوق الباب، وسَتَكون هناك خزانة واسعة فيها وِسادة سابِعة، لِأن هناك ستّ وَسائد على السرير الكبير.

1 Ghalib is a travelling sales rep. ☐
2 Today, Ghalib is in Dammam. ☐
3 Tomorrow, Ghalib flies to Riyadh. ☐
4 Ghalib thinks all hotel rooms look the same. ☐
5 Ghalib will take a train to Abha. ☐
6 There will be a total of six pillows in the room tomorrow. ☐

Activity 7
Now find the Arabic phrases below in what Ghalib says, as in the example.

a seventh pillow ٥	I'll fly to Abha ١
	سأطير إلى أبها
comfortable chairs ٦	the luxury hotel ٢
above the door ٧	I move from town to town ٣
a small fridge ٨	a sales representative ٤

Activity 8
Now describe your own apartment or house. Use the prompts below to get you started, but try to include as much detail of the furniture as you can including size, age, comfort, etc. Write down notes and then record yourself. Play the model to review your pronunciation. You can also write up your description using your notes. Show your work to an Arabic speaker if you can.

يَتَكَوَّنُ بَيْتنا من ... غُرَف، وهي: Our house consists of ... rooms which are:

نَسْتَأْجِر شَقَّتنا. شَقَّتنا في الطابِق الـ... . هناك/لَيْسَ هناك مِصْعَد.

We rent our apartment. Our apartment is on the ... floor. There is/there isn't a lift

المَطْبَخ/الحَمّام حَديث/تَقْليديّ/واسِع/فاخِر

The kitchen/bathroom is modern/traditional/spacious/luxurious

في غُرْفَة المَعيشة هناك/لَيْسَ هناك ...

In the living room there is (are)/there isn't (aren't) ...

7 Around town

Part 1: Core vocabulary

30

Arabic	Pronunciation	English	Write it yourself
مَدينة (مُدُن)	madīna (mudun)	town/city	_____
جامِعة (ات)	jāmiɛa (āt)	university	_____
مَدْرَسة (مَدارِس)	madrasa (madāris)	school	_____
شارِع (شَوارِع)	shāriɛ (shawāriɛ)	street	_____
جِسْر (جُسور)	jisr (jusūr)	bridge	_____
سوق (أسْواق)	sūq (asāq)	market	_____
مَحَطّة (ات)	maḥaṭṭa (āt)	station	_____
مَوْقِف (مَواقِف)	mawqif (mawāqif)	[bus] stop	_____
مَطْعَم (مَطاعِم)	maṭɛam (maṭāɛim)	restaurant	_____
مَسْجِد (مَساجِد)	masjid (masājid)	mosque	_____
مَطار (ات)	maṭār (āt)	airport	_____
فُنْدُق (فَنادِق)	funduq (fanādiq)	hotel	_____
يَمين	yamīn	right	_____
يَسار	yasār	left	_____
وَسَط المَدينة	wasaṭ al-madīna	city centre	_____
نَزَلَ/يَنْزِل	nazala/yanzil	to get off/alight	_____
أخَذَ/يَأْخُذ	akhadha/ya'khudh	to take	_____
رَكِبَ/يَرْكَب	rakiba/yarkab	to ride	_____

Around town

Pronunciation tip

The letter ق (*qāf*)

The sound of the letter ق (*qāf*) is similar to an English 'q' sound but produced further back in the throat, as if you are blowing a bubble at the back of your throat while saying 'q'. The word for market (or 'souk') ends with the letter ق (*qāf*): سوق *sūq*. It is also one of the letters in these Arab place names. Listen and repeat the Arabic pronunciation carefully.

قَطَر *qatar* Qatar   العِراق *al-irāq* Iraq

القاهِرة *al-qāhira* Cairo   مَسْقَط *musqat* Muscat

Activity 1

Match the English and the Arabic directions, for example ١c.

Go to the train station.	a	١ خُذْ أَوَّل شارِع على اليَمين.
How do I get to the centre of Muscat?	b	٢ اِرْكَبي الباص إلى الجِسر.
Take the first street on the right.	c	٣ أَيْنَ شارِع السوق؟
Get off at the university.	d	٤ اِذْهَبي إلى مَحَطّة القِطار.
Where's Market Street?	e	٥ وَسَط مَدينة مَسْقَط مِنْ أَيْنَ؟
Ride the bus to the bridge.	f	٦ اِنْزِلْ عِنْدَ الجامِعة.

Activity 2

Choose three places around town from the list. Ask for directions and give a response, using the phrases below. Practise out loud, listening to the model for help with pronunciation. You can record yourself and get some feedback from an Arabic speaker. When you are confident, write down your directions.

أَيْنَ ...؟ / ... مِنْ أَيْنَ؟   Where's .../How do I get to ...?

اِذْهَبْ، اِذْهَبي إلى ...   Go *(masc., fem.)* to ...

خُذْ، خُذي/ اِرْكَبْ، اِرْكَبي ...   Take *(masc., fem.)*/Ride *(masc., fem.)* ...

اِنْزِلْ، اِنْزِلي عِنْدَ ...   Get off *(masc., fem.)* at ...

_____

_____

_____

Activity 3

These characters are looking for work. Guide them to their most promising destinations.

Additional vocabulary

مَكْتَب البَريد post office

١ أنتَ مُدَرِّس؟ اِذهَب إلى ...
a المَدرَسة   b الجِسر   c الفُندُق

٢ أنتَ طَبّاخ؟ اِذهَب إلى ...
a الجامِعة   b المَحَطّة   c المَطعَم

٣ أنتِ مُمَرِّضة؟ اِذهَبي إلى...
a المَطار   b المُستَشفى
c مَكتَب البَريد

٤ أنتَ سائِق قِطار؟ اِذهَب إلى ...
a المَحَطّة   b الشارِع   c الفُندُق

٥ أنتُم مُوَظَّفون؟ اِذهَبوا إلى ...
a الفُندُق   b الجِسر   c الشارِع

٦ أنتِ مُحاسِبة؟ اِذهَبي إلى ...
a المَطعَم   b المُستَشفى
c البَنك

Activity 4

Hakim is talking about his daily working routine. First listen to what he says and write the missing words, as in the example.

أنا اسمي حكيم. أنا سائِق باص. أنا أعرِف كلّ ــــشارِعــــ في هذه المدينة الجميلة، وكلّ ـــــــــــ، وكلّ بيت. في الصباح، يركب بَعض الناس الباص، وهو في ـــــــــــ، قَبلَ أن أخرُج بِهِ إلى الشوارع. بَعدَ أن نَخرُج من ـــــــــــ المدينة، وبَعدَ ـــــــــــ الكبير، آخُذ طريق الملك حتّى مَوقِف ـــــــــــ. ينزِل الطَّلَبة والمُدَرِّسون هناك. بعد ذلك، آخُذ أوّل شارع على ـــــــــــ، لآخُذ المطار إلى محطّة ـــــــــــ، محطّة المُمَرِّضات والمُمَرِّضين! يَقول كلّ الناس: «ـــــــــــ يا عمّ حكيم!» وأنا أقول لَهُم، «مع السلامة يا أصدِقائي!»، ثُمَّ ـــــــــــ بالباص حتّى المطار.

Around town

Activity 5
A local magazine is doing a feature on Hakim. Help them by deciding if the statements below about Hakim and his bus route are true (T) or false (F).

☐ ١ حكيم هو سائِق باص في المدينة.

☐ ٢ هناك جامِعة في المدينة.

☐ ٣ المُستَشفى على طَريق المَطار.

☐ ٤ يذهَب حكيم إلى الجِسر الكبير قبلَ أن يخرُج من وَسَط المدينة.

☐ ٥ يأخُذ حكيم أوّل شارع على اليَسار بعد المُستَشفى.

☐ ٦ كلّ الناس يَعرِفون حكيم.

Part 2: Extension vocabulary

Arabic	Pronunciation	English	Write it yourself
عاصِمة (عَواصِم)	ɛāṣima (ɛawāṣim)	capital	_____
مَيْدان (مَيادين)	maydān (mayādīn)	roundabout/ square	_____
قَريب، أقْرَب	qarīb, aqrab	near, nearest	_____
طَريق (طُرُق)	ṭarīq (ṭuruq)	road	_____
قِسْم الشُّرْطة (أقْسام الشُّرْطة)	qism ash-shurṭa (aqsām ash-shurṭa)	police station	_____
رَصيف (أرْصِفة)	raṣīf (arṣifa)	pavement	_____
ناصية (نَواصٍ)	nāṣya (nawāṣin)	street corner	_____
عِمارة (ات)	ɛimāra (āt)	apartment block	_____
إشارة (ات) مُرور	ishārat (āt) murūr	traffic light	_____
مَشَى/يَمْشي	masha/yamshī	to walk	_____
سَألَ/يَسْألَ	sa'ala/yas'al	to ask	_____
(لا) يوجَد، (لا) توجَد	(lā) yūjad, (lā) tūjad	can(not) be found	_____

Activity 6

Read the story about Khadija and her search for a specific local restaurant. Fill in the blanks in the English summary below, as in the example.

نَزَلَتْ خديجة بَرَكات من غُرفَتِها الفاخِرة في فندق «قَصر النُّجوم»، وسَأَلَتْ عامِل المِصعَد الشابّ: "أين مَطعَم الفَنّانين من فضلك؟".
قالَ العامِل: "آسِف. أنا لا أعرِف. أنا لا أسكن هنا. اِسألي في مكتب البريد. المكتب قَريب جِدّاً من الفندق. أوّل شارع على اليَسار، قبلَ المَيدان."

دَخَلَتْ خديجة بَرَكات مكتب البريد، وسَأَلَت المُوَظَّف: "أين مَطعَم الفَنّانين من فضلك؟".
قالَ المُوَظَّف: "مَطعَم الفَنّانين؟ أنا سَمِعْتُ هذا الاسم، ولكن لا أعرِف في أيِّ شارع. اِسألي في قِسم الشُّرطة. القِسم بِجانب هذا المكتب على نَفس الرَّصيف، عند إشارة المُرور."

مَشَتْ خديجة على الرَّصيف نَحوَ إشارة المُرور، ثُمَّ دَخَلَتْ قِسم الشُّرطة، وقالَتْ للشُّرطيّ: "أين مَطعَم الفَنّانين من فضلك؟". قالَ الشُّرطيّ: "آسِف يا اِبنَتي. لا أعرِف هذا المَطعَم. اِسألي في فندق «قَصر النُّجوم». عامِل المِصعَد هناك ابن أُختي. هو سَيَعرِف!"

1 _Khadija_ Barakat was looking for *The Artists'* _____.

2 She was staying in a _____ called _____ of the _____.

3 First, she _____ the boy who operates the _____.

4 He suggested asking at the _____ office. 'Take the _____ street on the _____', he said, '_____ the square.'

5 So, next Khadija _____ the _____ at the _____, and he _____ _____ either.

6 By the _____ of the story, Khadija had gone a complete _____!

Around town

Activity 7
Now choose the best answers for the questions about Khadija's story.

١ مَن هي والِدة عامل المِصعَد؟
a أُخت خديجة   b والِدة خديجة   c أُخت الشُّرطيّ

٢ أين تسكُن خديجة بَرَكات وهي في هذه المدينة؟
a في فندق الفَنّانين   b في فندق قَصر النُّجوم   c في عِمارة النُّجوم

٣ إلى أين مَشَتْ خديجة بعدَ مكتب البَريد؟
a إلى الفندق   b إلى إشارة المُرور   c إلى أوّل شارع على اليَسار

٤ هل مكتب البَريد وقِسم الشُّرطة على رَصيف واحد؟
a لا   b لا نعرِف   c نعم

٥ كيف يعرف عامل المِصعَد الشُّرطيّ؟
a يَعمَل الشُّرطيّ في الفندق   b الشُّرطيّ هو خالُه
c عامل المِصعَد هو ابن الشُّرطيّ وخديجة

> **Language tip**
>
> **The town 'square'**
> The Arabic word مَيْدان *maydān* is often translated into English as 'square' in the context of a town or city, for example مَيْدان التَّحْرير *maydān at-taḥrīr*, 'Tahrir Square'. In reality the *maydān* is just as likely to be round as square. The word originates from 'ground' or 'battlefield', and has no connection to the shape of the feature.

Activity 8
Now talk about your home town. Use the prompts below to help you. Write down notes for your description first, and then record yourself. Play the model to review your pronunciation. You can also write up your description using your notes. Show your work to an Arabic speaker if you can.

أنا أَسْكُنْ في ... ... I live in

بَيْتي/عِمارَتي بِجانِب/أَمام/قَريب(ة) مِن ... ... My house/block is next to/in front of/near

في مَدينتي يوجَد/توجَد ... In my town ... can be found

ولكن لا يوجَد/لا توجَد ... But ... can't be found

آخُذ الـ... إلى المَكتَب/المَدرَسة/الجامِعة I take the ... to the office/school/university

أيّام الجُمعة/السَّبت/الأَحَد أذهب إلى ... ... On Fridays/Saturdays/Sundays, I go to

35

8 The world of education

Part 1: Core vocabulary

Arabic	Pronunciation	English	Write it yourself
طالِب (طُلّاب)	ṭālib (ṭullāb)	student	_____
تِلْميذ (تَلاميذ)	tilmīdh (talāmīdh)	pupil	_____
مُعَلِّم (ون)	muʿallim (ūn)	instructor, teacher	_____
دَرْس (دُروس)	dars (durūs)	lesson	_____
مَكْتَبة (ات)	maktaba (āt)	library	_____
صَفّ (صُفوف)	ṣaff (ṣufūf)	class, grade	_____
اِمْتِحان (ات)	imtiḥān (āt)	exam	_____
لُغة (ات)	lugha (āt)	language	_____
عِلْم (عُلوم)	ʿilm (ʿulūm)	science	_____
الرِّياضيّات	ar-riyāḍiyyāt	mathematics	_____
التاريخ	at-tārīkh	history	_____
الجُغْرافيا	al-jughrāfiyā	geography	_____
الرِّياضة	ar-riyāḍa	sport	_____
الموسيقى	al-mūsīqa	music	_____
الرَّسْم	ar-rasm	art/drawing	_____
التَّرْبية الدينيّة	at-tarbiya ad-dīnīyya	religious education	_____
قَرَأَ/يَقْرَأ	qara'a/yaqra'	to read	_____
تَعَلَّمَ/يَتَعَلَّم	taʿallama/yataʿallam	to learn	_____

The world of education

> **Language tip**
>
> Additional vocabulary relevant to the world of education has been presented in previous units. For example, in Unit 3 you will find the verbs 'to study' دَرَسَ/يَدْرُس (*darasa/yadrus*) and 'to write' كَتَبَ/يَكْتُب (*kataba/yaktub*). In Unit 5 you will find the word for 'teacher' مُدَرِّس (*mudarris*), and in Unit 7 the words for 'school' مَدْرَسة (*madrasa*) and 'university' جامِعة (*jāmiʿa*). This overlap of vocabulary themes occurs frequently, and it is always a good idea to review previous lists for relevant words.

Activity 1
Match the school subjects in the box to the picture clues, for example ١f.

٧ العُلوم	٤ الموسيقى	١ الرِّياضة
٨ اللُّغات	٥ القِراءة	٢ الرَّسْم
٩ التاريخ	٦ الرِّياضيّات	٣ الجُغْرافِيا

Activity 2
Read these highlights from your weekly schedule, then answer the Arabic questions below, as in the example.

جغرافيا	٨،٣٠ صباحاً	الثُّلاثاء
موسيقى	٢،٠٠ بعد الظُّهر	الإِثْنَيْن
رسم	٨،٣٠ صباحاً	السَّبْت
تاريخ	٩،١٥ صباحاً	الأَرْبِعاء
رياضيّات	١،٣٠ بعد الظُّهر	الأَحَد
علوم	١٠،١٥ صباحاً	الخَميس
لغة فَرَنسيّة	٩،٣٠ صباحاً	الجُمْعَة

١ في أيّ يَوْم تَدرُسون الموسيقى؟   يوم الاثنين _____

٢ في أيّ ساعة تَدرُسون الفَرَنسيّة؟ _____

٣ في أيّ يَوْم تَدرُسون الرسم؟ _____

٤ في أيّ ساعة تَدرُسون العلوم؟ _____

٥ في أيّ يَوْم تَدرُسون الجغرافيا؟ _____

٦ في أيّ ساعة تَدرُسون الرياضيّات؟ _____

Activity 3
Say something about your own education. Use these prompts to help you:

أنا كُنْتُ تِلميذاً (تِلميذة) في مَدْرَسة ...   I was a pupil at (a) ... school

أنا طالِب (طالِبة) في جامِعة ...   I am a student at (a) ... university

(كُنْتُ) أَدْرُس ... يَوْم الـ...   I (used to) study ... on ... day

(كُنْتُ) أُحِبّ ... ...   I (used to) like ...

(لا) أُجيد ... ...   I am (not) good at ...

Practise out loud, listening to the model for help with pronunciation. When you are confident, write down your description.

_____

_____

_____

Part 2: Extension vocabulary

Arabic	Pronunciation	English	Write it yourself
التَّعْلِيم/التَّرْبِية	at-taʿlīm/at-tarbiya	education	
كُلِّية (ات)	kulliyya (āt)	college, faculty	
مُحاضَرة (ات)	muḥāḍara (āt)	lecture	
أُسْتاذ (أَساتِذة)	ustādh (asātidha)	professor, lecturer	
دَوْرة (ات)	dawra (āt)	course	
مادّة (مَوادّ)	mādda (mawādd)	subject	
الهَنْدَسة	al-handasa	engineering	
الطِّبّ	aṭ-ṭibb	[study of] medicine	
الحُقوق	al-ḥuqūq	[study of] law	
رَوْضة (رِياض)	rawḍa (riyāḍ)	kindergarten	
اِبْتِدائِيّ	ibtidāʾī	primary	
إعْدادِيّ	iʿdādī	preparatory	
ثانَوِيّ	thānawī	secondary	
دَرَّسَ/يُدَرِّس	darrasa/yudarris	to teach	
عَلِمَ/يَعْلَم	ʿalima/yaʿlam	to know (a fact)	
عَلَّمَ/يُعَلِّم	ʿallama/yuʿallim	to instruct	
سَجَّلَ/يُسَجِّل	sajjala/yusajjil	to enrol	

🔍 Cultural tip

Schools in the Arab World are often divided into three core levels: اِبْتِدائِيّ (ibtidāʾī) 'primary' or 'elementary' (ages 5–11); إعْدادِيّ (iʿdādī) 'preparatory' (ages 12–14), also known as مُتَوَسِّط (mutawassiṭ) 'middle'; and ثانَوِيّ (thānawī) 'secondary' (ages 15–17). University courses are usually four years and students can be as young as 17 when they start.

Activity 4
Write the missing Arabic words in the sentences to match the English translation, as in the example.

English	Arabic
I am a student at secondary school.	١ أنا طالب في المدرسة <u>الثانوية</u>.
I left middle school last year.	٢ غادَرْتُ المدرسة _____ السَّنة _____.
I like Mondays.	٣ أنا _____ أيّام _____.
We study science in the morning.	٤ نحن _____ العُلوم في _____.
Majid prefers Tuesdays.	٥ _____ ماجد _____ الثُّلاثاء.
He likes reading history books.	٦ _____ أن _____ كُتُب _____.
I'd like to enrol my daughter in the faculty of medicine.	٧ _____ أن _____ اِبْنَتي في كُلِّيّة _____.
Majid hopes to enrol [himself] in the faculty of law.	٨ يأمَل _____ أن _____ نَفسَهُ في _____ الحُقوق.

Activity 5
Ibrahim is talking about his son, Faris. Read what he says, and then find the Arabic to match the English phrases at the top of page 43, as in the example.

أُريد أن أُسَجِّل ابني فارس لِيدرُس في كُلِّية الهَندَسة بجامعة «وارسو» في بولندا. أُريد من الأساتذة هناك أن يُعَلِّموه كيف تُصنَع الغَسّالات أو الثَّلاجات. أُريده أن يَتَعَلَّم كيف تعمَل المَصاعِد ومُكَيِّفات الهَواء في الأَبنِية الكبيرة. وبعد أن يرجع إلَيْنا وهو مُهندس كبير ومُهِمّ، سَيجِد عَمَلاً بسُرعة وبسُهولة في أيّ مَصنَع أو فُندُق هنا في مَدينَتِنا أو في أيّ مدينة قريبة. أو، رُبَّما، يعمَل كأُستاذ هنا ويُدَرِّس الهَندَسة لِأَبناء البَلَد!

The world of education

how elevators work	٥	the faculty of engineering	١
		كلّيّة الهندسة	
a big and important engineer	٦	Warsaw University	٢
quickly and easily	٧	the professors/the lecturers	٣
the youngsters in our country	٨	how washing machines are made	٤

Activity 6
Now read what Ibrahim says again and decide if the following sentences are true (T) or false (F).

1 Ibrahim wants his son, Faris, to study medicine. ☐

2 He hopes his son will be able to study in Poland. ☐

3 He wants him to learn practical skills. ☐

4 He hopes that Faris will stay and work in Poland after his studies. ☐

5 Ibrahim thinks his son will find work easily if he returns. ☐

6 He believes his son will maybe in turn teach the next generation. ☐

Activity 7
Describe your education and/or aspirations in detail. Use the prompts below and the vocabulary in this unit to get you started. Play the model to review your pronunciation. Write down notes and then record yourself, or present to a group. You can also write up your description using your notes. Show your work to an Arabic speaker if you can.

ما زِلْتُ في المدرسة/الكُلّيّة/الجامعة. .I am still at school/college/university

غادَرْتُ المدرسة/الكُلّيّة/الجامعة مُنْذُ ... .I left school/college/university ... ago

(كانَتْ) المَوادّ المُفَضَّلة عِندي في المدرسة/الكُلّيّة/الجامعة ...
My favourite subjects at school/college/univerity are (were) ...

أَدْرُسُ/دَرَسْتُ/أُريد أن أَدْرُس ... ... I am studying/studied/would like to study

أَعْتَقِد أنَّ المُحاضَرات/الدَّوْرة/الدُّروس (كانَتْ) ... جِدّاً.
I think the lectures/the course/the lessons are (were) very ...

9 The Arab World

Part 1: Core vocabulary

🎧 40

Arabic	Pronunciation	English	Write it yourself
الشَّرْق الأَوْسَط	ash-sharq al-awsaṭ	The Middle East	_____
مِصْر/مِصْرِيّ	miṣr/miṣrīy	Egypt/Egyptian	_____
لُبْنان/لُبْنانيّ	lubnān/lubnānīy	Lebanon/Lebanese	_____
سوريا/سوريّ	sūriyā/sūrīy	Syria/Syrian	_____
العِراق/عِراقيّ	al-ɛirāq/ɛirāqīy	Iraq/Iraqi	_____
السَّعوديّة/سَعوديّ	as-saɛūdīyya/saɛūdīy	Saudi [Arabia]/Saudi	_____
الأُرْدُنّ/أُرْدُنّيّ	al-urdunn/urdunnīy	Jordan/Jordanian	_____
أَمْريكا/أَمْريكيّ	amrīkā/amrīkīy	America/American	_____
بِريطانْيا/بِريطانيّ	biriṭānyā/biriṭānīy	Britain/British	_____
بَلَد (بِلاد)	balad (bilād)	country	_____
عاصِمة (عَواصِم)	ɛāṣima (ɛawāṣim)	capital	_____
شَمال	shamāl	north	_____
جَنوب	janūb	south	_____
شَرْق	sharq	east	_____
غَرْب	gharb	west	_____
سافَرَ/يُسافِر	sāfara/yusāfir	to travel	_____
زارَ/يَزور	zāra/yazūr	to visit	_____
نَزَلَ/يَنْزِل	nazala/yanzil	to stay (at a hotel, etc.)	_____

The Arab World

Language tip

Countries and nationalities

You can see a pattern in the Arab countries and nationalities, with the country name often starting with *al-* ('the'), and the nationality ending with the sound *-īy*. Here are some more Arab countries and nationalities that will immediately sound familiar to you. Listen and repeat the Arabic pronunciation.

قَطَر *qaṭar* Qatar   الكُوَيْت *al-kuwayt* Kuwait

قَطَريّ *qaṭarīy* Qatari   كُوَيْتيّ *kuwaytīy* Kuwaiti

البَحْرَيْن *al-baḥrayn* Bahrain   الإمارات *al-imārāt* The Emirates

بَحْرَيْنيّ *baḥraynīy* Bahraini   إماراتيّ *imārātīy* Emirati

Activity 1

Each of the following has a specific purpose for travel. Match the purpose to the appropriate destination.

I want to visit Abu Dhabi and Dubai. ٤   I want to visit Baghdad. ١

a الأردنّ b الإمارات c لبنان   a السعوديّة b سوريا c العراق

I want to visit Buckingham Palace. ٥   I want to visit the Pyramids. ٢

a أمريكا b البحرين c بريطانيا   a لبنان b بريطانيا c مصر

I want to visit Hollywood. ٦   I want to visit Mecca and Medina. ٣

a مصر b أمريكا c الكويت   a السعوديّة b قطر c أمريكا

Activity 2

Say where you are from and where you have travelled. Use the prompts below to help you. Don't forget to listen to the model for help with pronunciation and to record yourself. When you are confident, write down what you said.

أنا مِن ...   I'm from ...

سافَرْتُ إلى ... (السَّنة الماضية/مُنْذُ ...)   (Last year/... ago) I travelled to ...

ولَكِنّي ما زُرْتُ ...   But I didn't visit ...

_____

_____

_____

_____

Activity 3

Alex is talking about his study trip to the Middle East. Look at the cities and the sites they visited below. Think about which place fits in each gap in what Alex says. Then listen and write in the answers, as in the example.

الأهْرام The Pyramids	عَمّان Amman	أَسْوان Aswan
الأُقْصُر Luxor	القاهِرة Cairo	طيبة Thebes
The Valley of the Kings وادي المُلوك	البَتْراء Petra	The West Bank [of Nile] البَرّ الغَرْبيّ
	وادي رُم Wadi Rum	

نَحنُ طَلَبة أمريكيّون. نَدرُس التاريخ ونُحِبّ قِراءة الكُتُب القديمة. في الشَّهر الماضي، سافَرْنا إلى <u>القاهِرة</u> في مصر، ونَزَلْنا في فُنْدُق كبير أمام _____. بَعدَ ذلك، زُرْنا _____ في الجَنوب، ثُمَّ أَخَذْنا المَركَب إلى الشَّمال لنَذهَب إلى _____. في البَرّ _____ من النَّهر، جَلَسْنا بجانِب مَعْبَد فِرْعونيّ، وتكَلَّمَ الأساتِذة عَن وادي _____، وعَن _____ وهي العاصِمة القديمة. بَعدَ ذلك أَخَذْنا الطائرة وسافَرْنا إلى الأردُنّ. هناك، زُرْنا مدينة _____، و _____ رُم و _____. نحن تَعَلَّمْنا الكثير في هذه الرِّحْلة، وسَنَرجِع إلى _____ الأوْسَط في السنة القادمة وسَنَزور بِلاداً أُخرى!

Activity 4

Now read your completed transcript of what Alex says and decide if the following sentences are true (T) or false (F).

1. We visited Luxor, then we visited Aswan. ☐
2. We flew to the city of Amman in Jordan. ☐
3. We are Arab students who visited America. ☐
4. Our lecturers spoke to us about the Valley of the Queens. ☐
5. We are studying history. ☐
6. Last year, we visited Egypt. ☐
7. Next year, we will return to visit more countries. ☐

Part 2: Extension vocabulary

Arabic	Pronunciation	English	Write it yourself
ليبْيا/ليبيّ	lībyā/lībīy	Libya/libyan	
السودان/سودانيّ	as-sūdān/sūdānīy	Sudan/Sudanese	
عُمان/عُمانيّ	ʿumān/ʿumānīy	Oman/Omani	
اليَمَن/يَمَنيّ	al-yaman/yamanīy	Yemen/Yemeni	
تونِس/تونِسيّ	tūnis/tūnisīy	Tunisia/Tunisian	
الجَزائِر/جَزائِريّ	al-jazā'ir/jazā'irīy	Algeria/Algerian	
المَغْرِب/مَغْرِبيّ	al-maghrib/maghribīy	Morocco/Moroccan	
رِحْلة (ات)	riḥla (āt)	journey	
السِّياحة	as-siyāḥa	tourism	
مُسافِر (ون)	musāfir (ūn)	tourist/traveller	
الحَجّ	al-ḥajj	the pilgrimage	
جِنْسيّة (ات)	jinsīyya (āt)	nationality	
سِفارة (ات)	sifāra (āt)	embassy	
تَأْشيرة (ات)	ta'shīra (āt)	visa	
غادَرَ/يُغادِر	ghādara/yughādir	to leave	
وَصَلَ/يَصِل	waṣala/yaṣil	to arrive	
أدّى/يُؤَدّي	adda/yu'addī	to undertake	

> **Language tip**
>
> Wherever you travel in the Middle East, you will hear local dialects specific to the region. You may not fully understand the Arabic spoken on the street, and in the course of your studies you will probably want to gain a more detailed knowledge of at least one dialect. However, Modern Standard Arabic is a universal key that can act as a gateway to these dialects, and also to Arab culture and history in general.

Activity 5

You have seen these Arabic jobs advertised online. Look at the ads and then find the Arabic words and phrases to match the English below, as in the example.

Additional vocabulary

مُغادَرة departure(s)   إدارة administration   مِنْطَقة region

---

مَطلوب لِلعَمَل

تُعلِن الشركة العربيّة للسَفَر والسِّياحة عن الوَظائف التالية:

مَندوبون لِلمَبيعات	لِلعَمَل في مَكاتبنا في البِلاد الآتية: العراق، اليمن، السودان [احفظ]
مُدير لِمنطَقة شَمال إفريقيا	الجِنسيّة: واحدة من بِلاد المغرب العربيّ: تونس، أو الجزائر، أو المغرب [احفظ]
مُدير لِرحلات الحَجّ	إدارة التأشيرات مع السفارات السعوديّة إدارة الوُصول والمُغادرة في المطارات [احفظ]
مُدير لِمنْطَقة أوروبا	مُدير لِرحلات السِّياحة في عَواصِم بِلاد غَرب أوروبا: باريس ولندن ومدريد وروما [احفظ]

---

١ nationality	٥ employees	٩ one of
جنسيّة		
٢ visas	٦ arrival(s)	١٠ capital cities
٣ embassies	٧ Western Europe	١١ wanted
٤ manager	٨ North Africa	١٢ Rome

The Arab World

Language tip

The 'Maghrib'
The Arabic word مَغْرِب *maghrib* literally means 'place where the sun goes down' and is connected to the words for 'sunset', غُروب *ghurūb*, and 'west', غَرب *gharb*. The phrase المَغْرِب العَرَبيّ *al-maghrib al-ɛarabīy*, 'The Arab Maghrib', refers to the whole of Arab north-west Africa. By itself, المَغْرِب *al-maghrib* usually refers only to the country of Morocco.

Activity 6

Now look again at the Arabic jobs on page 48. Select the appropriate Arabic phrase for each of the statements below.

١ The company that needs new staff operates in the area of:

a المُسْتَشْفيات b السَّفَر والسِّياحة c المدارس والجامعات

٢ The prefered nationality of the North Africa regional manager is:

a سوريّ أو لبنانيّ أو عراقيّ b مصريّ أو سودانيّ أو ليبيّ
c تونسيّ أو جزائريّ أو مغربيّ

٣ The company needs new sales reps in:

a ليبيا، الجزائر، مصر b لُنْدُن، مدريد، روما c العراق، اليمن، السودان

٤ The head of pilgrimage operations will work closely with:

a السِّفارات السعوديّة b الجامعات السعوديّة c السِّفارات الفَرَنسيّة

٥ The Western European capitals covered include:

a وارسو، أوسلو، دُبلِن b لُنْدُن، مدريد، روما c أثينا، برلين، ستوكهولم

Activity 7

Describe a recent journey. Use the prompts below to help you, and try to include as much of the vocabulary in this unit as you can. Play the model to review your pronunciation. Write down notes and then record yourself, or present to a group. You can also write up your description using your notes.

45

(Last year/... ago) I visited ... with ...   زُرْتُ ... مع ... (السَّنة الماضية/مُنْذُ ...)

We took visas from the ... embassy   أَخَذْنا تَأْشيرات مِن السِّفارة الـ...

We left ... and travelled by ... to ...   غادَرْنا ... وسافَرْنا بِالـ... إلى ...

We stayed in a ... near ...   نَزَلْنا في ... قَريب مِن ...

We went to ... in the ... of the country   ذَهَبْنا إلى ... في ... البَلَد.

The journey was very ...   كانَت الرِّحلة ... جِدّاً.

10 Shopping

Part 1: Core vocabulary

46

Arabic	Pronunciation	English	Write it yourself
التَّسَوُّق	at-tasawwuq	shopping	_____
مَحَلّ (ات)	maḥall (āt)	shop, store	_____
تاجِر (تُجّار)	tājir/tujjār	trader, merchant	_____
سِعْر (أَسْعار)	siɛr (asɛār)	price	_____
لَوْن (أَلْوان)	lawn (alwān)	colour	_____
مَقاس (ات)	maqās (āt)	size	_____
وَزْن (أَوْزان)	wazn (awzān)	weight	_____
كِيس (أَكْياس)	kīs (akyās)	bag, sack	_____
مَصْنوع مِن	maṣnūɛ min	made of	_____
ذَهَب	dhahab	gold	_____
فِضّة	fiḍḍa	silver	_____
نُحاس	nuḥās	copper	_____
جِلْد	jild	leather	_____
خَشَب	khashab	wood	_____
قُطْن	quṭn	cotton	_____
حَرير	ḥarīr	silk	_____
بِكَمْ؟	bi-kam?	how much?	_____
اِشْتَرى/يَشْتَري	ishtara/yashtari	to buy	_____
باعَ/يَبيع	bāɛa/yabīɛ	to sell	_____

Shopping

Language tip

Words to describe colour

The basic Arabic colours follow a pattern, for example أَبْيَض *abyaḍ* 'white', and أَخْضَر *akhḍar* 'green', which become بَيْضاء *bayḍā'* and خَضْراء *khaḍrā'* for feminine or plural items. You can also expand your repertoire of colours into more subtle areas by adding an *-īy* ending to items of that colour. Listen to these examples:

لَيْمون *laymūn* lemons → لَيْموني *laymūnīy* lemon-yellow

زَيْتون *zaytūn* olives → زَيْتوني *zaytūnīy* olive-green

رَماد *ramād* ashes → رَمادي *ramādīy* grey, ashen

Activity 1

Read what Maha says in English about her village market. Then match the Arabic phrases to the pictures, for example ١c.

"In our village square, Saturday is shopping day. There's an open market where you can buy almost anything! I bought my best ring there – 24-carat gold, they told me! My sister even bought a lemon-yellow silk kimono in this market. There's a trader from China who sells them in many colours and sizes. He also has cotton ones, but the price is less for cotton. My mother is planning on buying a grey bag there next Saturday, and my aunt will look for a wooden table."

٥ سِعره أغلى	١ كيمونو لَيْموني من الحَرير
٦ مائدة مَصْنوعة من الخَشَب	٢ أمّي وخالَتي
٧ يوم السَّبت القادِم	٣ حقيبة رَماديّة لأمّي
٨ تاجِر من الصين	٤ خاتم ذَهَبيّ

Activity 2
Now complete these Arabic sentences to match what you have learnt about Maha's village market, as in the example.

Additional vocabulary

قَرْيَة village   القادِم next   بَحَثَ/يَبْحَث عَن to look for

١ يوم السَّبت هو يوم ‎_‎__السوق‎__‎_ في قَرْيَتنا.

٢ اِشْتَرَتْ ‎_____‎ كيمونو ‎_____‎
مَصنوع من ‎_____‎.

٣ سَتَبْحَث خالَتي عن ‎_____‎ مَصنوعة من ‎_____‎.

٤ سَتَشْتَري أمّي ‎_____‎ رَماديّة يوم ‎_____‎ القادِم.

٥ تاجِر الكيمونو من ‎_____‎.
يَبيع الكيمونو بِـ ‎_____‎ و ‎_____‎ كثيرة.

٦ في السوق، ‎_____‎ خاتِمي المَصنوع ‎_____‎ الذَّهَب.

Activity 3

🎧 48

Imagine you want to go to the market in Maha's village to buy a particular item. Prepare some requests and questions using these prompts.

I'd like to buy ...	أُريد أن أشْتَري ...
Is this made of ...?	هَل هذا (هذه) مَصْنوع(ة) مِن ...
How much is this one?	بِكَم هذا (هذه)؟
Do you have something bigger/cheaper?	هَل عِندَكُم شَيْء أكْبَر/أرْخَص؟
Do you have other colours/sizes?	هَل عِندَكُم ألْوان/مَقاسات أُخْرى؟

Practise out loud, listening to the model for help with pronunciation. When you are confident, write down your description.

_____

_____

_____

_____

Part 2: Extension vocabulary

Arabic	Pronunciation	English	Write it yourself
مَرْكَز التَّسَوُّق (مَراكِز التَّسَوُّق)	markaz at-tasawwuq (marākiz at-tasawwuq)	shopping centre, shopping mall	
بائِع (ون)	bā'iɛ (ūn)	seller	
تَخْفيض (ات)	takhfīḍ (āt)	discount	
عَرْض (عُروض)	ɛarḍ (ɛurūḍ)	offer	
تَوْصيل (ات)	tawṣīl (āt)	delivery	
حِساب (ات)	ḥisāb (āt)	account	
سَلّة (سِلال)	salla (silāl)	basket	
تاريخ الشِّراء	tārīkh as-shirā'	purchase date	
مَلابِس، أَزْياء	malābis, azyā'	clothes	
أَثاث	athāth	furniture	
صوف	ṣūf	wool	
بلاسْتيك	blāstīk	plastic	
وَرَق	waraq	paper	
طَلَبَ/يَطْلُب	ṭalaba/yaṭlub	to order	
بَحَثَ/يَبْحَث	baḥatha/yabḥath	to search	
جَرَّبَ/يُجَرِّب	jarraba/yujarrib	to try (on), to test	
فاصَلَ/يُفاصِل	fāṣala/yufāṣil	to barter, to haggle	

🔍 Cultural tip

Even if you can't go to a market or mall in the Arab World, there are still many interesting online shopping sites in the Middle East selling perfume, clothes, furniture and more. You can select the Arabic language option and wander around these websites at home.

Activity 4

Youssef is ordering from an online clothing retailer, *Spring Clothing*. First, look at the website and match the Arabic to the English.

a my order	e my account	١ عَرض خاصّ ٥ سَلّة
b basket	f special offer	٢ قُمْصان ٦ تَخْفيضات
c hats	g discounts	٣ طَلَبي ٧ قُبَّعات
d search	h shirts	٤ اِبْحَث ٨ حِسابي

Activity 5

50

Youssef is now calling customer services at *Spring Clothing* and speaks to an agent called Samira. Listen to their conversation and read the transcript below. Then answer the questions about the conversation on page 55.

سميرة: أزياء الرّبيع. صباح الخير. معك سميرة.

يوسف: صباح الخير. أنا اسمي يوسُف حِجازي. عندي حِساب معكم. اِشتَرَيْتُ قُبَّعة خضراء على الإنترنت.

سميرة: هل هناك مُشكِلة في المَقاس؟ في اللون؟

يوسف: لا. أنا لَم أُجَرِّب القُبَّعة لأنَّها لَم تَصِل بَعد.

سميرة: هل اِشتَرَيْتَ القُبَّعة في أُسبوع تخفيضات الرّبيع؟

يوسف: لا أعرِف. كان هناك عَرض خاصّ على سِعر هذه القُبَّعات المَصنوعة من القُطن أو الصوف. أنا قُبَّعَتي خضراء وقُطنيّة.

سميرة: ما هو رَقم السَّلّة وتاريخ الشِّراء؟ سَأبحَث عَنها على الكمبيوتر.

يوسف: رَقم السَّلّة ٨٨ ت، وتاريخ الشِّراء الاثنين.

سميرة: الاثنين؟ ولكن اليوم الثُّلاثاء. هل اِشتَرَيْتَها أمس يا سَيِّد حِجازي؟

يوسف: نعم.

سميرة: تَناوَل إفطارك يا سَيِّد حِجازي. القُبَّعة في الطَّريق إلَيْك!

Shopping

1 What day of the week does the conversation take place?
2 What has Youssef bought from the online retailer, *Spring Clothing*?
3 What is his problem with the order?
4 Does Youssef have an account with the retailer?
5 What basket number and sales date does he quote?
6 What suggestion does Samira have for Youssef, and why?

Activity 6
Now read the conversation again and choose the appropriate phrase to complete the sentence.

١ تَعمَل سميرة في ...
a مَصنَع أحذِيَة   b بيت حِجازي
c مَحَلّ أزياء الرَّبيع

٢ اِشتَرى يوسف قُبَّعَته من ...
a الإنترنت   b سَلّة سميرة
c سوق القَريَة

٣ قُبَّعة يوسف لَوْنها...
a أصفر   b أزرق   c أخضر

٤ قُبَّعة يوسف مَصنوعة من ...
a الصوف   b القُطن   c الجِلد

٥ القُبَّعة ...
a وَصَلَت أمس   b سَتَصِل اليوم
c وَصَلَت اليوم

٦ تَرى سميرة أن يوسف عَلَيْه ...
a الانتِظار قَليلاً   b أن يَأتي إلى المَصنَع   c أن يَختار لَوْناً مُختَلِفاً

٧ هاتَفَ يوسف سميرة صباح ...
a الاِثنين   b الثُّلاثاء   c الأربِعاء

٨ هناك عَرض خاصّ على سِعر ...
a الأزياء   b القُبَّعات   c الصوف

Activity 7
Talk about your shopping preferences and some items that you have bought recently. Use the prompts below and the vocabulary in this unit to get you started. Try to include opinions and reasons for your preferences. Play the model to review your pronunciation. You can also write up your talk using your notes. Present your work to an Arabic speaker if you can.

أُحِبّ أن أشتَري ... في السوق/مَركَز التَّسَوُّق.   I like to buy ... in the market/the mall.

ولكنّي أُفَضِّل أن أشتَري ... على الإنترنت.   But I prefer to buy ... on the Internet.

(لا) أُحِبّ أن أُفاصِل مَعَ البائِع.   I (don't) like to bargain with the seller.

أمس/الأسبوع الماضي، اِشتَرَيْتُ ... و....   Yesterday/Last week, I bought ... and ....

هناك عُروض خاصّة/تَخفيضات على الأسعار.
There are special offers/discounts on the prices.

11 Food and drink

Part 1: Core vocabulary

52

Arabic	Pronunciation	English	Write it yourself
طَعام (أطْعِمة)	ṭaɛām (aṭɛima)	food	_____
حِساب (ات)	ḥisāb (āt)	bill, check	_____
بَقّالة (ات)	baqqāla (āt)	grocery	_____
مَخْبَز (مَخابِز)	makhbaz (makhābiz)	bakery	_____
خَضْرَوات، خُضَريّ	khaḍrawāt, khuḍarī	vegetables, greengrocer	_____
لَحْم، لَحّام	laḥm, laḥḥām	meat, butcher	_____
سَمَك، سَمّاك	samak, sammāk	fish, fishmonger	_____
دَجاج	dajāj	chicken	_____
فَواكِه	fawākih	fruit	_____
خُبْز	khubz	bread	_____
حَليب	ḥalīb	milk	_____
شاي	shāy	tea	_____
قَهْوَة	qahwa	coffee	_____
ماء	mā'	water	_____
عَصير	ɛaṣīr	juice	_____
أَكَلَ/يَأْكُل	akala/ya'kul	to eat	_____
شَرِبَ/يَشْرَب	shariba/yashrab	to drink	_____
دَفَعَ/يَدْفَع	dafaɛa/yadfaɛ	to pay	_____
جَهَّزَ/يُجَهِّز	jahhaza/yujahhiz	to prepare	_____

56

Food and drink

Cultural tip

Be careful in the market!
The names of individual fruits and vegetables can vary from region to region in the Arab World. There is no 'standard' Arabic word for tomatoes, variously known as طماطم *ṭamāṭim*, بندورة *banadūra*, or قوطة *qūṭa*. Likewise, 'peaches' are known as خوخ *khawkh* or درّاق *durrāq*. The word خوخ *khawkh* can also refer to 'plums', which in other regions are known as برقوق *barqūq*.

Activity 1
What do I need? Choose the best answer according to what I want to do.

١ أريد أن أُجَهِّز ساندَوِتش.
a عصير   b خبز   c شاي

٢ أريد أن أشتري خبزاً.
a حليب   b دجاج   c مخبز

٣ أريد أن أُجَهِّز الطعام.
a مطبخ   b حساب   c شاي

٤ أريد أن أُجَهِّز السَّلَطة.
a قهوة   b حليب   c خضروات

٥ أريد أن أدفَع.
a مطابخ   b حساب   c حليب

٦ أريد أن أشرَب عصيراً.
a فواكه   b لحم   c سمك

٧ أريد أن أغسل وجهي.
a قهوة   b بقّالة   c ماء

٨ أريد أن أشتري دجاجة.
a مخبز   b لحّام   c خضريّ

Activity 2
Match the words with the pictures, for example ١d. Can you pronounce the words without their vowels?

١ الفواكه
٢ الدجاجة
٣ الشاي
٤ الحساب
٥ السمك
٦ الخبز
٧ قَهوَتي
٨ الخضروات

Activity 3

Now choose one of the words in Activity 2 on page 57 and write it in the gap, as in the example.

١ اِشْتَرَيتُ هذا ____الخِبز____ من المخبز.

٢ هذه _____. سَأَشْرَبُها الآن.

٣ هَل اِشتَرَيتَ هذه _____ من الخُضَريّ؟

٤ شَرِبنا عصير _____ في هذا المحلّ.

٥ اِشْتَرَيت هذا _____ من السمّاك.

٦ دَفَعوا _____ لصاحِبة المحلّ.

٧ اِشْتَرَتْ أمّي هذا _____ من البقّالة.

٨ اِشْتَرى أبي هذه _____ من اللحّام.

Activity 4

53

Imagine you want to go to town to buy some food and have a snack in a café. Prepare some requests and questions using these prompts.

English	Arabic
I'd like to buy ... from the ...	أُريد أن أَشْتَري ... من الـ...
We'd like to drink/to eat ...	نُريد أن نَشرَب/أن نَأكُل ...
Do you have ...?	هَل عِندَكُم ...؟
Can I have (half) a kilo of ...?	مُمكِن (نِصف) كيلو ...؟
How much is the bill?	كَم الحِساب؟

Practise out loud, listening to the model for help with pronunciation. When you are confident, write down what you said.

Part 2: Extension vocabulary

Arabic	Pronunciation	English	Write it yourself
إفْطار	ifṭār	breakfast	_____
غَداء	ghadā'	lunch	_____
عَشاء	ᶜashā'	dinner	_____
فُرْن (أفْران)	furn (afrān)	oven	_____
طَبَق (أطْباق)	ṭabaq (aṭbāq)	dish, plate	_____
كوب (أكْواب)	kūb (akwāb)	glass	_____
سِكّين (سَكاكين)	sikkīn (sakākīn)	knife	_____
شَوْكة (شُوَك)	shawka (shuwak)	fork	_____
مِلْعَقة (مَلاعِق)	milᶜaqa (malāᶜiq)	spoon	_____
سَلَطة (ات)	salaṭa (āt)	salad	_____
مَشْويّ	mashwī	grilled	_____
مَقْليّ	maqlī	fried	_____
مَحْشيّ	maḥshī	stuffed	_____
مَفْروم	mafrūm	minced	_____
مَسْلوق	maslūq	boiled	_____
مُقَطَّع	muqaṭṭaᶜ	chopped	_____
تَناوَل/يَتَناوَل	tanāwala/ yatanāwal	to eat, to partake	_____

Cultural tip

Some dishes and drinks are common to the entire Middle East. For example, varieties of the following can be found throughout the region: ورق عنب waraq ᶜinab 'stuffed vine leaves' (literally 'grape leaves'), فلافل falāfil 'falafel', باذنجان مخلّل bādhinjān mukhallil 'pickled aubergine', حمّص ḥummuṣ 'chick peas', طحينة ṭaḥīna 'tahini', سلطة الزبادي salaṭat az-zabādī 'yoghurt salad', and شاي بالنعناع shāy bin-naᶜnāᶜ 'tea with mint'.

Activity 5

Zaid and Dina's engagement party is next Thursday. Dina's mother has made a list of dishes for all the family to prepare.

Additional vocabulary

كَرَفْس celery   خَلّ vinegar   جَمبَريّ prawns   حَساء soup

> **أطباق لحَفل خُطوبة زيد ودينا**
> - ثلاث دجاجات مسلوقة للحَساء، مع الفِلفِل الأسود
> - ثلاث دجاجات مطبوخة في الفرن مع البطاطس والثوم
> - ثلاث سمكات مشوية، وثلاث مقلية، مع الأرزّ بالبَصَل الأحمر
> - ورق عنب وباذنجان محشي باللحم المفروم
> - خمس سلطات في خمسة أطباق:
>   - الطماطم المقطَّعة مع الجُبن والزيت
>   - الحمّص مع الزَّيتون والخيار
>   - الجَمبَريّ مع الخَلّ والليمون
>   - الجَزَر مع الكَرَفس والزَّبيب
>   - الزبادي مع النَّعناع والثوم

Dina's mother is looking through the list of dishes and deciding what they need to buy from each shop. Complete her table below with the items needed, as in the examples.

البقّالة	الخضريّ	السمّاك	اللحّام
فِلفِل أسود (black pepper)			٦ دجاجات (6 chickens)

Food and drink

Activity 6
55 Hassan lives a busy life. Listen to what he says about his eating habits and see if you can hear and read the Arabic phrases below in what he says, as in the example.

> أنا أعيش وأعمَل في مدينة كبيرة. أتَناوَل إفطاري واقِفاً، وأتَناوَل غدائي بِسُرعة، جالِساً على مكتبي. أما عشائي فأتَناوَلهُ في مطعم، أو أشتري وَجبة جاهِزة وآكُلها في البيت. مطبخي نظيف جِدّاً! فيه بَعض الأكواب المصنوعة من البوليستيرين، وشُوَك وملاعق وسكاكين وأطباق مصنوعة من البلاستك.

English	#		English	#
a ready meal	٥		I eat my breakfast	١
			أتناول إفطاري	
I eat it in the house	٦		standing up	٢
made from polystyrene	٧		sitting down at my desk	٣
made from plastic	٨		as for my dinner	٤

Activity 7
56 Talk about your eating habits. Use the prompts below and Activity 6 to help you. Play the model to review your pronunciation. You can also write up your talk using your notes. Present your work to an Arabic speaker if you can.

أنا أعيش وأعمَل في ... ...   I live and work in ...
أشتَري طَعامي مِن ... ...   I buy my food from ...
أتَناوَل إفطاري/غَدائي/عَشائي ... ...   I eat my breakfast/lunch/dinner ...
كُلّ يَوم، أُجَهِّز عَشائي في ... ...   Every day, I prepare my dinner in ...
وَجبَتي المُفَضَّلة هي ... ...   My favourite meal is ...
أنا (لا) آكُل وَجَبات جاهِزة كَثيراً   I (don't) eat ready meals much

12 Going out

Part 1: Core vocabulary

57

Arabic	Pronunciation	English	Write it yourself
أَوَّلاً	awwalan	firstly	_____
أَخيراً	akhīran	finally	_____
ثُمَّ	thumma	then	_____
قَبْلَ/بَعْدَ ذَلِكَ	qabla/baɛda dhālika	before/after that	_____
الطَّقْس	aṭ-ṭaqs	the weather	_____
مُشْمِس	mushmis	sunny	_____
مُمْطِر	mumṭir	rainy	_____
غائِم	ghā'im	cloudy	_____
مَتْحَف (مَتاحِف)	matḥaf (matāḥif)	museum	_____
حَديقة (حَدائِق)	ḥadīqa (ḥadā'iq)	park	_____
سينِما (سينِمات)	sīnima (sīnimāt)	cinema	_____
مَسْرَح (مَسارِح)	masraḥ (masāriḥ)	theatre	_____
صَديق (أَصْدِقاء)	ṣadiq (aṣdiqā')	friend	_____
شاهَدَ/يُشاهِد	shāhada/yushāhid	to watch, to view	_____
قابَلَ/يُقابِل	qābala/yuqābil	to meet	_____
حَجَزَ/يَحْجِز	ḥajaza/yaḥjiz	to reserve	_____
ضَحِكَ/يَضْحَك	ḍaḥika/yaḍḥak	to laugh	_____
اِسْتَمْتَعَ/يَسْتَمْتِع بِ	istamtaɛa/yastamtiɛ bi-	to enjoy	_____

Going out

Activity 1
Choose the best drawing to complete the sentences.

Activity 2
Use the prompts below to invite a friend to go out with you. You can include more than one activity using the connecting words and phrases in the list opposite. Listen to the model for help with pronunciation and don't forget to try and record yourself. When you are confident, write down what you said.

The weather is ... today.	الطَّقْس ... اليَوْم.
Would you like to go to the ...?	هَل تُريد(ين) أن تَذْهَب(ي) إلى الـ....؟
I have reserved to see ... at the ...	حَجَزْتُ لِأُشاهِد ... في الـ....

_____

_____

_____

_____

Activity 3

59

Shukri and his wife, Zahra, are being interviewed for a documentary about how couples met. Listen to the interview, reading the Arabic transcript. Then complete the English translation below, as in the example.

شُكري: أنا مِصريّ، وأعمَل في مَتحَف كبير، واسمي شُكريّ.

زَهرة: وأنا زَهرة. أنا مُمَثِّلة في المَسرَح.

شُكري: في صباح مُمطِر، قابَلْتُ زَهرة على سُلَّم المَسرَح.

زَهرة: كُنْتُ أمشي بِسُرعة نَحوَ الباب وهو كانَ مع كَلبه، تيتو.

شُكري: قُلْتُ لَها: "لِماذا تَمشين بِسُرعة، والطقس مُمطِر، والماء في كلّ مَكان؟!"

زَهرة: قُلْتُ لَهُ: "أَوَّلاً، نَتعارَف! ما اسم ... هذا الكلب الجميل؟"

شُكري: ضَحِكْنا، وبَعدَ ذلك أصبَحْنا أصدِقاء، أنا وهي وتيتو!

زَهرة: اِستَمتَعْنا مَعاً بالمَشي في الحَدائق، ومُشاهَدة الأفلام في السينما.

شُكري: وأخيراً، تَزَوَّجْنا مُنذُ عِشرين سَنة!

Shukri: I'm _Egyptian_. I work in a large _____. My name is Shukri.

Zahra: And I'm Zahra. I'm an actress in the _____.

Shukri: One _____ morning. I _____ Zahra on the steps of the _____.

Zahra: I was _____ quickly towards the _____ and he was with his _____, Tito.

Shukri: I _____ to her: "Why are you walking quickly when the _____ is rainy and the _____ is everywhere?!".

Zahra: I _____ to him: "_____, let's get aquainted! What's the name of ... this _____ dog?".

Shukri: We _____, and _____ that we became _____, me and her and Tito!

Zahra: We both _____ walking in the _____ and watching films in the _____.

Shukri: And _____, we got married _____ years ago.

Part 2: Extension vocabulary

Arabic	Pronunciation	English	Write it yourself
ريف (أرْياف)	rīf (aryāf)	countryside	
صَحْراء (صَحارى)	ṣahrā' (ṣahāra)	desert	
مِنْطَقة (مَناطِق)	minṭaqa (manāṭiq)	region, area	
جَبَل (جِبال)	jabal (jibāl)	mountain	
قَلْعة (قِلاع)	qalʿa (qilāʿ)	fort, castle	
واحة (ات)	wāḥa (āt)	oasis	
نَخْلة (نَخيل)	nakhla (nakhīl)	palm tree	
شاطِئ (شَواطِئ)	shāṭi' (shawāṭi')	beach	
بَحْر (بِحار)	baḥr (biḥār)	sea	
طَبيعيّ	ṭabīʿīy	natural	
صَحْراويّ	ṣaḥrāwīy	desert-like	
ريفيّ	rīfīy	rustic, rural	
رَأى/يَرى	ra'a/yara	to see	
شَمَّ/يَشُمّ	shamma/yashumm	to smell	
قاد/يَقود (سَيّارة)	qāda/yaqūd (sayyāra)	to drive (a car)	
سَبَحَ/يَسْبَح	sabaḥa/yasbaḥ	to swim	
تَوَجَّهَ/يَتَوَجَّه (نَحْوَ)	tawajjaha/yatawajjah (naḥwa)	to head (towards)	

> **Language tip**
>
> Names of places in the Middle East can have specific meanings in Arabic. For example, the Arabic for Bahrain, البحرين *al-bahrayn*, literally means 'the two seas'. Likewise the Sahara Desert comes from the Arabic word for 'deserts', صحارى *ṣahāra*. Sometimes these familiar connections can help you to retain vocabulary.

> **Language tip**
>
> **Verbal nouns**
> Nouns are formed from verbs in English by adding endings such as *-ing*, *-tion*, or *-ment*. In Arabic, verbal nouns also follow patterns but these are changes within the word based on the root letters rather than endings. The verbal noun patterns vary for basic verbs. For example, ذَهاب *dhahāb* 'going' from the verb ذَهَبَ/يَذهَب *dhahāba/yadh-hab* 'to go'; or جُلوس *julūs* 'sitting' from the verb جَلَسَ/يَجلِس *jalasa/yajlis* 'to sit'. However, the verbal noun patterns are largely predictable for the forms (or variations) of the verb. For example, تَجْهيز *tajhīz* 'preparation' from the verb جَهَّزَ/يُجَهِّز *jahhaza/yujahhiz* 'to prepare', or إدارة *idāra* 'management/administration' from the verb أدارَ/يُدير *adāra/yudīr* 'to manage/to administer'. A good dictionary will show the verbal nouns alongside the verbs.
>
> It is common in Arabic to use a verbal noun following an initial verb, so it is useful to understand how they work. Look at the following ways of expressing the same meaning, using two verbs or a verbal noun:
>
> أُحِبّ أن أذهَب إلى السينما. / أُحِبّ الذَهاب إلى السينما.
> (I like to go to the cinema.)
>
> نُفَضِّل أن نَجلِس في المَقْهى. / نُفَضِّل الجُلوس في المَقْهى.
> (We prefer to sit in the café.)

Activity 4
Match the verbs with the relevant nouns, for example ١f.
Then write the English meanings next to the Arabic.

قِيادة	a _____	١ سَبَحَ/يَسْبَح	_to swim_
حَجْز	b _____	٢ قابَلَ/يُقابِل	_____
مُشاهَدة	c _____	٣ تَوَجَّهَ/يَتَوَجَّه	_____
زِيارة	d _____	٤ قادَ/يَقود	_____
شَمّ	e _____	٥ اِسْتَمْتَعَ/يَسْتَمْتِع	_____
سِباحة	f _swimming_	٦ شاهَدَ/يُشاهِد	_____
ضَحِك	g _____	٧ شَمَّ/يَشُمّ	_____
اِسْتِماع	h _____	٨ حَجَزَ/يَحْجِز	_____
مُقابَلة	i _____	٩ زارَ/يَزور	_____
تَوَجُّه	j _____	١٠ ضَحِكَ/يَضْحَك	_____

Going out

Activity 5

Amir is Tunisian. He is telling a friend in an email about what he likes to do in his time off. Look at the email and then answer the questions below. Don't worry about understanding every word. Concentrate on getting the gist.

Additional vocabulary

winter الشِّتاء   summer الصَّيْف   holidays عُطلات   pleasant لَطيف

1. How does Amir describe the weather in Tunisia?
2. Does Amir like to go abroad for his holidays?
3. Why does he like to go to the beaches in summer?
4. What does he like to do in the rural areas?
5. Why does he head for desert regions in winter?
6. What does Amir look at while walking in the mountains?

Activity 6

Talk about how you like to spend your time off. Use the prompts below and Amir's email to help you. Write down notes first, and then record yourself. Play the model to review your pronunciation. You can also write up your description using your notes. Show your work to an Arabic speaker if you can.

في ... ، الطَّقس دائماً ... و...   In ..., the weather is always ... and ...

أنا أُحِبّ أن أقضي عُطلاتي ...   I like to spend my holidays ...

في الصَّيف/الشِّتاء، أتَوَجَّه نَحوَ ...   In the summer/the winter, I head for ...

أسْتَمْتِع بِزيارة ...   I enjoy visiting ...

أمشي/أقود سَيّارَتي في الـ... لأُشاهِد ...   I walk/I drive in the ... to look at ...

13 Everyday life

Part 1: Core vocabulary

Arabic	Pronunciation	English	Write it yourself
كُلّ يَوْم	kull yawm	every day	_____
دائماً	dā'iman	always	_____
عادةً	ɛādatan	usually	_____
أَحْياناً	aḥyānan	sometimes	_____
أيّام الـ...	ayyām al...	on ... days	_____
الساعة ...	as-sāɛa ...	at ... o'clock	_____
الساعة...والنِّصْف	as-sāɛa ... wan-niṣf	at half past ...	_____
الساعة ... والرُّبْع	as-sāɛa ... war-rubɛ	at quarter past ...	_____
الساعة ... والثُّلْث	as-sāɛa ... wath-thulth	at twenty ('a third') past ...	_____
دَقيقة (دَقائِق)	daqīqa (daqā'iq)	minute	_____
مَتى؟	mata?	when?	_____
حالة (ات)	ḥāla (āt)	state, condition	_____
صَحا/يَصْحو	ṣaḥa/yaṣḥū	to wake up	_____
نامَ/يَنام	nāma/yanām	to sleep	_____
لَبِسَ/يَلْبَس	labisa/yalbas	to wear, to put on	_____
غَسَلَ/يَغْسِل	ghasala/yaghsil	to wash	_____
لَعِبَ/يَلْعَب	laɛiba/yalɛab	to play	_____
خَرَجَ/يَخْرُج	kharaja/yakhruj	to leave, to go out	_____

Everyday life

63

> **Language tip**
>
> **Telling the time**
> When you're telling the time in standard Arabic, you need to use the 'ordinal' numbers (first, second, third, etc.), rather than the 'cardinal' numbers (one, two, three, etc.). Listen to these examples:
>
> الساعة الخامسة *as-sā ͽa al-khāmisa* five o'clock (literally 'the fifth hour')
>
> الساعة الثالثة والنِّصف *as-sā ͽa al-thālitha wan-niṣf* half-past three (literally 'the third hour and the half')
>
> الساعة العاشِرة والثُّلث *as-sā ͽa al-ͽāshira wath-thulth* twenty past ten (literally 'the tenth hour and the third')
>
> الساعة الواحِدة وسِتّ دَقائق *as-sā ͽa al-wāḥida wa sitt daqā'iq* six minutes past one (literally 'the first hour and six minutes')

Activity 1

Choose the clock which shows the correct time, for example ۱b.

۱ الساعة الرابِعة	a	b	c
۲ الساعة الثامِنة	a	b	c
۳ الساعة الثانية والنِّصف	a	b	c
٤ الساعة الخامِسة والنِّصف	a	b	c
٥ الساعة التاسِعة والرُّبع	a	b	c
٦ الساعة السادِسة والرُّبع	a	b	c
۷ الساعة التاسِعة والثُّلث	a	b	c
۸ الساعة العاشِرة وخَمس دَقائق	a	b	c
۹ الساعة الرابِعة وعَشَر دَقائق	a	b	c

Activity 2
Write the missing Arabic words in the sentences to match the English translation, as in the example.

English	Arabic
Every day, I wake up at half past seven.	١ كلّ يوم، ___أَصْحو___ الساعة _____ والنصف.
After that I wash my face.	٢ بَعدَ ذلك _____ وَجهي.
I look out of the window to see what the weather is like.	٣ أنظُر من _____ لِأرى حالة _____.
I usually have breakfast at eight o'clock.	٤ _____ أتَناوَل إفطاري الساعة _____.
Sometimes I do ('I play') some light exercise.	٥ أحياناً _____ بَعضَ الرياضة _____.
I leave the house at quarter past nine.	٦ _____ من البيت الساعة التاسعة و_____.

Activity 3
Talk about your morning routine. Use the prompts below to say what you do in the mornings. You can vary the order or how often you do certain things.

English	Arabic
Every day I wake up at ...	كلّ يوم أصْحو الساعة ...
I always ...	أنا دائماً ...
I sometimes ...	أنا أحياناً ...
I eat my breakfast at ...	أتَناوَل إفطاري الساعة ...
I usually leave the house at ...	عادةً أخْرُج من البَيت الساعة ...

Practise out loud, listening to the model for help with pronunciation. When you are confident, write down what you said.

_____

_____

_____

_____

_____

Part 2: Extension vocabulary

Arabic	Pronunciation	English	Write it yourself
عادة (ات)	ɛāda (āt)	routine, habit	
نادِراً	nādiran	rarely	
لا ... أَبَداً	lā ... abadan	never	
طَوالَ ...	ṭawāla ...	all ... long	
حَوالَيْ	ḥawālay	about, approximately	
وَجْه (وُجوه)	wajh (wajūh)	face	
سِنّ (أَسْنان)	sinn (asnān)	tooth	
ذَقْن (ذُقون)	dhaqn (dhuqūn)	chin	
شَعْر	shaɛr	hair	
اِسْتَيْقَظَ/يَسْتَيْقِظ	istayqaẓa/yastayqiẓ	to get up	
نَظَّفَ/يُنَظِّف	naẓẓafa/yunaẓẓif	to clean	
رَتَّبَ/يُرَتِّب	rattaba/yurattib	to tidy	
أَعَدَّ/يُعِدّ	aɛadda/yuɛidd	to prepare, to get ready	
حَلَقَ/يَحْلِق	ḥalaqa/yaḥliq	to shave	
وَقَفَ/يَقِف	waqafa/yaqif	to stand	
فَكَّرَ/يُفَكِّر	fakkara/yufakkir	to think	
نَسِيَ/يَنْسى	nasiya/yansa	to forget	

> **Language tip**
>
> In Arabic, you cannot simply 'shave'. You need to add the area that you are shaving, most commonly the 'chin'. So the phrase 'I shave before breakfast' would become 'I shave my chin before breakfast':
>
> أحلِق ذَقني قَبلَ الإفطار ahliq daqnī qabla l-ifṭār.

Activity 4

Nur has produced a commentary about her morning routine for her fitness instructor. Read the first part of her commentary and pick out the Arabic equivalents of the phrases below, as in the example.

Additional vocabulary

حَسَبَ according to   غَلّاية ماء kettle   جُزْء part   يَوْمِيّات diary

---

يَوْمِيّات نور: الجُزْء الأوّل

**الساعة السادسة إلى الساعة السادسة و ٣٠ دقيقة،
أو ٣٢ دقيقة - حَسَبَ البَيضة المَسلوقة**

كلّ يوم، أصحو الساعة السادسة وأتَوَجَّه نحوَ غَلّاية الماء في المطبخ. بعد ذلك أتَوَجَّه نحوَ الحمّام لِأغسِل وَجهي، وأنظُر من شبّاك الحمّام لِأرى حالة الطَّقس في هذا الصباح. ثمّ أرجِع إلى المطبخ لِأُجَهِّز كوب الشاي الأوّل. أقِف في وَسَط المطبخ وأُفَكِّر في إفطاري، وفي حالة الطَّقس، وملابسي لِليوم. بعد ذلك، أخرُج من المطبخ وأتَوَجَّه نحوَ غُرفة الطعام ومعي الشاي وأي طعام يُقابِلني بين وَسَط المطبخ والمائدة. عادةً أتَناوَل إفطاري في حوالَيْ خمس دقائق وأحياناً في سبع، إذا كانَ في طَبَقي بَيضة مَسلوقة.

---

١ I head towards
<u>أتوجّه نحو</u>

٢ the bathroom window
_____

٣ what the weather is like
_____

٤ the first glass of tea
_____

٥ I think about my breakfast
_____

٦ any food that encounters me
_____

٧ if there is
_____

٨ a boiled egg
_____

Everyday life

Activity 5
Nur's commentary continues. Read the second part and decide if the sentences below are true (T) or false (F).

يَوْمِيّات نور: الجُزء الثاني
الساعة السادسة و٣٠ دقيقة ، أو ٣٢ دقيقة إلى الساعة السابعة والربع

أنا لا أشرَب القهوة أبَداً. ولِذلك، أرجِع إلى غُرفة نومي بَعدَ الإفطار لِأُرَتِّبها قليلاً، ولِأُعِدّ ما سَألبَسه اليوم فوقَ سريري. نادِراً، ألعَب بَعضَ الرياضة الخفيفة، ولكنّي عادةً أنسى. بعد ذلك، أرجِع إلى الحمّام لِأُنَظِّف أسناني، ولِأغسِل شَعري. وقَبلَ أن أخرُج من الحمّام، أنظُر من الشبّاك لِأرى حالة الطقس مَرّة أُخرى. وأخيراً، أشكُر الله لأنّي سَيِّدة ولا أحتاج إلى أن أحلِق ذَقني كلّ صباح مِثل أبي وأخي! أخرُج من البيت الساعة السابعة والربع.

1 Nur's morning routine lasts an hour and a quarter in total. ☐

2 She always drinks coffee in the morning. ☐

3 She lays the clothes she will wear on her bed in the morning. ☐

4 Nur often works out in the morning. ☐

5 She sometimes forgets to clean her teeth. ☐

6 She looks at the weather from the window twice during the morning. ☐

7 Unlike her father and brother, Nur doesn't need to shave every morning. ☐

8 She leaves the house at half past seven. ☐

Activity 6
Write a commentary about your own evening routine. Use Nur's commentary and the words and phrases in this unit to help you. You could deliver the commentary as a presentation. Include videos/photos if you can. Show your work to a native speaker or post it in an online forum if you're feeling brave.

14 Society and current affairs

Part 1: Core vocabulary

66

Arabic	Pronunciation	English	Write it yourself
مُجْتَمَع (ات)	mujtamaع (āt)	society	_____
حُكومة (ات)	ḥukūma (āt)	government	_____
صِناعة (ات)	ṣināعa (āt)	industry	_____
دين (أَدْيان)	dīn (adyān)	religion	_____
حَياة (حَيَوات)	ḥayāh (ḥayawāt)	life	_____
مُسْتَقْبَل	mustaqbal	future	_____
صِحّة	ṣiḥḥa	health	_____
سَعادة	saعāda	happiness	_____
اِقْتِصاد	iqtiṣād	economy	_____
مَلِك (مُلوك)	malik (mulūk)	king	_____
أَمير (أُمَراء)	amīr (umarā')	emir, prince	_____
وَزير (وُزَراء)	wazīr (wuzarā')	minister	_____
رَئيس (رُؤَساء)	ra'īs (ru'asā')	president, head	_____
شَعْب (شُعوب)	shaعb (shuعūb)	people, populace	_____
عيد (أَعْياد)	عīd (aعyād)	feast, festival	_____
جَميع	jamīع	every, everyone	_____
بَنى/يَبْني	bana/yabnī	to build	_____
ساعَدَ/يُساعِد	sāعada/yusāعid	to help, to assist	_____
اِسْتَقْبَلَ/يَسْتَقْبِل	istaqbala/yastaqbil	to receive (guests, etc.)	_____

Society and current affairs

Activity 1

Match the singular words with their plurals, for example ۱c. Then write the English meanings, as in the example.

صِناعات	a _____	مَلِك	۱	_king_
أديان	b _____	حُكومة	۲	_____
مُلوك	c _kings_	وَزير	۳	_____
مُجتَمَعات	d _____	عيد	٤	_____
وُزَراء	e _____	شَعب	٥	_____
حُكومات	f _____	صِناعة	٦	_____
شُعوب	g _____	دين	۷	_____
أعياد	h _____	مُجتَمَع	۸	_____

> **! Language tip**
>
> **Uncountables**
> Some words such as صِحّة ṣiḥḥa 'health' and سَعادة saʿāda 'happiness' do not have a commonly used plural. As in English, they are 'uncountable'.
>
> صِحّة أُمّي ṣiḥḥat ummī the health of my mother
> صِحّة أُمَّهاتِنا ṣiḥḥat ummahātinā the health of our mothers
>
> سَعادة الشَّعب saʿādat ash-shaʿb the happiness of the people
> سَعادة كُلّ شُعوب saʿādat kull shuʿūb the happiness of all peoples

Activity 2

Express your views and opinions about society. Use the prompts below to help you. Don't forget to listen to the model for help with pronunciation and record yourself. When you are confident, write down what you said.

أَعْتَقِد/في رَأيي ...   I think/In my opinion ...

أَهَمّ شَيْء في الحَياة هو ...   The most important thing in life is ...

عَلَيْنا أن نَبْني/نُساعِد ...   We should build/help ...

_____

_____

_____

Activity 3

The Prime Minister's office has sent out the messages below on social media in the past few days. Each message reflects one of these general themes:
- public holiday
- general inspiration
- visiting dignitaries
- the economy

Choose a theme and write it next to the appropriate message below.

Activity 4
Now complete the translations of the messages, as in the example.

1. Special ___thanks___ to the Minister of the _____ who has _____ me. Our _____ is strong and is growing every _____!

2. Happy _____ on the occasion of _____ Day. _____ and _____ to all the _____!

3. I _____ a group of _____ today. The _____ is bright for _____!

4. The _____ is working for _____ seven _____ a week. Together we will _____ a better _____!

Society and current affairs

Part 2: Extension vocabulary

Arabic	Pronunciation	English	Write it yourself
اِنْتِخاب (ات)	intikhāb (āt)	election	_____
قانون (قَوانين)	qānūn (qawānīn)	law	_____
ثَقافة (ات)	thaqāfa (āt)	culture	_____
تَقْليد (تقاليد)	taqlīd (taqālīd)	tradition	_____
عَقْل (عُقول)	ɛaql (ɛuqūl)	mind, reason	_____
حَرْب (حُروب)	ḥarb (ḥurūb)	war	_____
سَلام	salām	peace	_____
مَناخ	manākh	climate	_____
مُؤَسَّسة خَيْرِيّة (مُؤَسَّسات خَيْرِيّة)	mu'assasa khayrīyya (mu'assasāt khayrīyya)	charity ('charitable institution')	_____
مُفيد	mufīd	beneficial	_____
ضارّ	ḍārr	harmful	_____
فَقير (فُقَراء)	faqīr (fuqarā')	poor (person)	_____
نَبيل (نُبَلاء)	nabīl (nubalā')	noble (person)	_____
مَريض (مَرْضى)	marīḍ (marḍa)	sick (person)	_____
مُسِنّ (ون)	musinn (ūn)	elderly (person)	_____
شَجَّعَ/يُشَجِّع	shajjaɛa/yushajjiɛ	to encourage	_____
تَطَوَّعَ/يَتَطَوَّع	taṭawwaɛa/yataṭawwaɛ	to volunteer	_____
اِحْتَفَلَ/يَحْتَفِل بِـ	iḥtafala/yaḥtafil bi-	to celebrate	_____
تَبَرَّعَ/يَتَبَرَّع	tabarraɛa/yatabarraɛ	to donate	_____

> **Language tip**
>
> **Making nouns into adjectives**
> The *-īy* ending (*nisba*), employed to create different colours (see page 52), can be used generally to make adjectives from a wide variety of nouns. For example, أسبوعيّ *usbūʿīy* 'weekly' from أسبوع *usbūʿ* 'week'; or خيريّ *khayrīy* 'charitable' from خير *khayr* 'charity, good works'.
>
> Remember to remove any *tā' marbūṭa* ending from the noun before adding the *-īy* ending. For example, حكوميّ *ḥukūmīy* 'governmental' from حكومة *ḥukūma* 'government'.

Activity 5
Using the vocabulary lists in this unit (pages 74 and 77) and the Language tip above, create Arabic adjectives that match the English below, as in the example.

legal ١	religious ٤	popular ٧
قانونيّ		
economic ٢	industrial ٥	healthy ٨
cultural ٣	traditional ٦	mental, rational ٩

Activity 6
Farida is a speaker at a rally organised by 'The Community Party'. She is young and doesn't have children, but is very interested in volunteering and charity work. Look at Farida at the rally and then read the slogans at the top of page 79 that she sees around her on the rally banners and posters. Which three messages do you think would interest Farida most?

Society and current affairs

☆ التَّبَرُّع للمُؤَسَّسات الخَيريّة من التَّقاليد الجميلة في بِلادنا

☆ الأسرة تُشَجِّع الأطفال على تَعَلُّم كلّ ما هو مُفيد

☆ حينَ نَحتَفِل بالأعياد يَجِب أن نَتَذَكَّر الفَقير والمَريض والمُسِنّ

☆ السَّلام أفضَل من الحُروب في بِناء مُستَقبَل الشُّعوب

☆ العَمَل التَّطَوُّعيّ يَبني الشَّخصيّة النَّبيلة

☆ العِلم والثَّقافة غِذاء للعَقل السَّليم

Activity 7
Look again at the Arabic slogans above that Farida saw at the rally. Select the appropriate Arabic phrase to complete each of the statements below.

١ We should remember the poor, the sick and the old when:
a نَحتَفِل بالصِّحّة   b نَحتَفِل بالأعياد   c نُساعِد الحُكومة

٢ Peace is better than war in building:
a مُستَقبَل التَّطَوُّع   b شَخصيّات الشُّعوب   c مُستَقبَل الشُّعوب

٣ One of the great traditions of our country is:
a التَّبَرُّع للمُؤَسَّسات التَّقليديّة   b التَّبَرُّع للمُؤَسَّسات العَقليّة   c التَّبَرُّع للمُؤَسَّسات الخَيريّة

٤ Everything beneficial children learn is encouraged by:
a الأُسرة   b الإنتِخابات   c الحُكومة

٥ Knowledge and culture are food for:
a العَقل النَّبيل   b العَقل السَّليم   c الأُسرة السَّليمة

٦ The noble character is built by:
a العَمَل التَّطَوُّعيّ   b العَقل التَّطَوُّعيّ   c العَمَل الصِّناعيّ

Activity 8
Have a go at producing some of your own slogans and messages. Use the examples in this unit to help you. You could illustrate the slogans as posters or format your messages for social media. Include videos/photos if you can. Show your slogans and messages to a native speaker, send them to any Arabic-speaking friends, or post them online. It's a good way of communicating in Arabic to the wider world. You might even get some replies!

Answers to activities

Unit 1

Activity 1

١ أَنا أَحْمَد. ٢ أَنا سَحَر. ٣ نَحْنُ حَمْدي وَمُحَمَّد. ٤ هَلْ أَنْتِ سَحَر؟ ٥ هَلْ أَنْتَ حَمْدي؟ ٦ مُحَمَّد هُناكَ.

Activity 2

١ أَنا مُحَمَّد. ٢ هِيَ سَحَر. ٣ هَلْ أَنْتَ أَحْمَد؟ ٤ هَلْ أَنْتِ سَحَر؟ ٥ نَحْنُ هُنا. ٦ هَلْ أَنْتُمْ هُنا؟ ٧ هَلْ هُمْ هُناكَ؟ ٨ أَنا حَمْدي وهوَ أَحْمَد.

Activity 3

١d; ٢k; ٣i; ٤b; ٥h; ٦l; ٧g; ٨c; ٩e; ١٠f; ١١a; ١٢j

Activity 4

١T; ٢F; ٣T; ٤F; ٥F; ٦T

Unit 2

Activity 1

١ هَذا ٢ هَذِهِ ٣ هَذا ٤ هَذا ٥ هَذِهِ ٦ هَذا ٧ هَذِهِ ٨ هَذِهِ

Activity 2

Order of the conversation (from top to bottom).

٢ ← ٣ ← ٦ ← ١ ← ٤ ← ٥

Activity 3

١ ما ٢ أَيْنَ ٣ كَيْفَ ٤ مَنْ ٥ هَلْ ٦ ما

Activity 4

هَذِهِ هِيَ دَرّاجَتي الجَديدة.
اِسْمُها "الريشة". ذَلِكَ لِأَنَّ دَرّاجَتي سَريعة وَجَميلة وخَفيفة مِثل الريشة!
هَذِهِ هِيَ قِصّة اِسْم دَرّاجَتي!

Unit 3

Activity 1

١ كَتَبَتْ سَميحة اِسمها. ٢ هَذا الجَمَل مِن السَّعوديّة. ٣ العُلْبة فَوْقَ المائِدة. ٤ يَجْلِس الكَلْب بَيْنَ الحَقيبَتَيْن. ٥ مَنْ أَكَلَ السَّمَكة؟ ٦ المِفْتاح تَحْتَ الكُرْسيّ. ٧ السَّيّارة عِنْدَ الخَيْمة.

Activity 2

١b; ٢h; ٣f; ٤a; ٥i; ٦c; ٧j; ٨d; ٩e; ١٠g

Activity 3

١ إلى الجامِعة ٢ بالمِتْرو ٣ بَعْدَ الجِسْر ٤ بِجانِب الشُّبّاك ٥ على الهاتِف ٦ فَوْقَ مَكْتَب ٧ قَريب مِن الجامِعة ٨ بالدَّرّاجة ٩ بِدَرّاجَتي السَّريعة

Unit 4

Activity 1

١d; ٢g; ٣a; ٤e; ٥b; ٦c; ٧f

Activity 2

There is a model recording numbered 16 on the audio.

Activity 3

Activity 4

١c; ٢b; ٣a; ٤c; ٥a; ٦a

Activity 5

١ My <u>parents</u> live with my <u>grandmother</u>.
٢ My <u>grandfather</u> said that he goes to the park with his <u>grandchildren</u> every day.
٣ My <u>cousins</u> work together <u>in</u> a carpet factory.
٤ My <u>fiancée</u> and I will visit her <u>family</u> in the village of 'Palace of Palms'.
٥ The life of my <u>(paternal) aunt</u> is hard because she is <u>divorced</u> and her <u>children</u> are young.
٦ My <u>(maternal) uncle</u> paid all the expenses of the wedding of my older <u>sister</u>.

Activity 6

١T; ٢F; ٣T; ٤F; ٥F; ٦F; ٧T; ٨T

Activity 7

There is a model recording numbered 18 on the audio.

Unit 5

Activity 1

١ نَجّار ٢ مُصَوِّر ٣ طَبّاخ ٤ فَنّان ٥ خَبّاز ٦ طَبيب

Activity 2

١b; ٢c; ٣a; ٤a; ٥b; ٦b

Activity 3

مدير/مساعد/مهندسين/مهندسين/عمّال/موظّفين

1 assistant manager and chief engineer
2 a thousand
3 24 hours a day
4 behind the factory
5 in a small palace next to the sea
6 yes, because Mohammed lives next to the sea and (we assume) also near the factory.

Activity 4

There is a model recording numbered 21 on the audio.

Activity 5

١T; ٢F; ٣T; ٤F; ٥T; ٦T

Activity 6

١j (yaƐmal); ٢d (daƐīfa); ٣h (sā'iq); ٤e (aƐmal); ٥a (sharika); ٦g (qawīya); ٧i (rawātib); ٨f (taƐmal); ٩b (maḥall); ١٠c (li-bayƐ)

Activity 7

٧:٣٠ ص	اجتماع مع <u>المحاسب</u>
٩:٣٠ ص	اجتماع مع كلّ <u>المَندوبين</u>
٢:٠٠ م	زِيارة <u>المَصنَع</u> الجديد
٥:٠٠ م	<u>محلّ</u> الورد
٦:٠٠ م	زِيارة <u>مديرة المَبيعات في المستشفى</u>

Activity 8

There is a model recording numbered 24 on the audio.

Unit 6

Activity 1

١ أَريكة ٢ باب ٣ سَجّادة ٤ سَرير ٥ وِسادة ٦ كُرْسيّ

Activity 2

١e؛ ٢d؛ ٣f؛ ٤a؛ ٥c؛ ٦b

Activity 3

١ السرير الصغير في الغرفة الصغيرة ٢ الخزانة الكبيرة بجانب الأريكة ٣ الثلّاجة بجانب باب المطبخ ٤ السرير الكبير والكراسي في غرفة النوم ٥ كلّ الوسائد على السرير الكبير ٦ الفرن بين الشبّاك والباب

Activity 4

There is a model recording numbered 27 on the audio.

Activity 5

١f؛ ٢e؛ ٣c؛ ٤a؛ ٥b؛ ٦d؛ ٧g

Activity 6

1T; 2T; 3F; 4T; 5F; 6F

Activity 7

١ سأطير إلى أبها ٢ الفُندُق الفاخِر ٣ أَنْتَقِل من مدينة إلى مدينة ٤ مَندوب مَبيعات ٥ وِسادة سابِعة ٦ كَراسي مُريحة ٧ فوق الباب ٨ ثلّاجة صغيرة

Activity 8

There is a model recording numbered 29 on the audio.

Unit 7

Activity 1

١c; ٢f; ٣e; ٤a; ٥b; ٦d

Activity 2

There is a model recording numbered 32 on the audio.

Activity 3

١a; ٢c; ٣b; ٤a; ٥a; ٦c

Activity 4

أنا اسمي حكيم. أنا سائق باص. أنا أعرِف كلّ <u>شارِع</u> في هذه المدينة الجميلة، وكلّ <u>مدرسةٍ</u>، وكلّ بيت. في الصباح، يركَب بَعض الناس الباص، وهو في <u>الموقِف</u>، قَبلَ أن أخرُج بِهِ إلى الشوارع. بَعدَ أن نَخرُج من <u>وسطِ</u> المدينة، وبَعدَ <u>الجِسرِ</u> الكبير، آخُذ طريق الملك حتّى مَوقِف <u>الجامعةِ</u>. ينزل الطَلَبة والمُدَرِّسون هناك. بعد ذلك، آخُذ أوّل شارع على <u>اليمين</u>، لآخُذ طريق المطار إلى محطّة <u>المستشفى</u>، محطّة المُمَرِّضات والمُمَرِّضين!

يَقول كلّ الناس: «<u>شكراً</u> يا عمّ حكيم!» وأنا أقول لَهُمْ، «مع السلامة يا أَصْدِقائي!»، ثُمَّ <u>أذهبُ</u> بالباص حتّى المطار.

Activity 5

١T; ٢T; ٣T; ٤F; ٥F; ٦T

Activity 6

1 <u>Khadija</u> Barakat was looking for *The Artists' <u>Restaurant</u>*.
2 She was staying in a <u>hotel</u> called *Palace of the <u>Stars</u>*.
3 First, she <u>asked</u> the boy who operates the <u>elevator</u>.
4 He suggested asking at the <u>post</u> office. 'Take the <u>first</u> street on the <u>left</u>', he said, '<u>before</u> the square.'
5 So, next Khadija <u>asked</u> the <u>employee</u> at the <u>post</u> <u>office</u>, and he <u>didn't</u> <u>know</u> either.
6 By the <u>end</u> of the story, Khadija had gone a complete <u>circle</u>!

Activity 7

١c; ٢b; ٣b; ٤c; ٥b

Answers to activities   85

Activity 8
There is a model recording numbered 35 on the audio.

Unit 8

Activity 1
١f; ٢e; ٣c; ٤g; ٥h; ٦i; ٧a; ٨d; ٩b

Activity 2
١ يوم الاثنين ٢ ٩،٣٠ صباحاً ٣ يوم السبت ٤ ١٠،١٥ صباحاً ٥ يوم الثلاثاء ٦ ١،٣٠ بعد الظهر

Activity 3
There is a model recording numbered 37 on the audio.

Activity 4
١ أنا طالب في المدرسة الثانوية.
٢ غادَرْتُ المدرسة المتوسّطة السَّنة الماضية.
٣ أنا أُحِبّ أيّام الاثنين.
٤ نحن ندرُس العُلوم في الصباح.
٥ يفضّل ماجد أيّام الثُّلاثاء.
٦ يُحِبّ أن يقرأ كُتُب التاريخ.
٧ أريد أن أُسجِّل ابنَتي في كُلِّيّة الطبّ.
٨ يأمَل ماجد أن يُسجِّل نَفسَهُ في كُلِّيّة الحُقوق.

Activity 5
١ كُلِّيّة الهندسة ٢ جامعة «وارسو» ٣ الأساتِذة ٤ كيف تُصنَع الغَسّالات ٥ كيف تعمَل المَصاعِد ٦ مُهندس كبير ومُهِمّ ٧ بسُرعة وبسُهولة ٨ أبناء البَلَد

Activity 6
١F; ٢T; ٣T; ٤F; ٥T; ٦T

Activity 7
There is a model recording numbered 39 on the audio.

Unit 9

Activity 1
١c; ٢c; ٣a; ٤b; ٥c; ٦b

Activity 2
There is a model recording numbered 42 on the audio.

Activity 3

نَحنُ طَلَبة أمريكيّون. نَدرُس التاريخ ونُحِبّ قِراءة الكُتُب القديمة. في الشَّهر الماضي، سافَرْنا إلى <u>القاهرة</u> في مصر، ونَزَلْنا في فُنْدُق كبير أمام <u>الأهرام</u>. بَعدَ ذلك، زُرْنا <u>أسوان</u> في الجَنوب، ثُمَّ أَخَذْنا المَركَب إلى الشَّمال لنَذهَب إلى <u>الأُقصُر</u>. في البَرّ <u>الغَربيّ</u> من النَّهر، جَلَسْنا بجانِب مَعْبَد فِرْعونيّ، وتَكَلَّمَ الأساتِذة عَن وادي المُلوك، وعَن <u>طيبة</u> وهي العاصِمة القديمة. بَعدَ ذلك أَخَذْنا الطائرة وسافَرْنا إلى الأُردُنّ. هناك، زُرْنا مدينة <u>عَمّان</u>، و<u>وادي رُم</u> و<u>البَتراء</u>. نحن تَعَلَّمْنا الكثير في هذه الرِّحْلة، وسَنَرجِع إلى <u>الشَّرْق</u> الأَوْسط في السنة القادمة وسَنَزور بِلاداً أُخرى!

Activity 4

1F; 2T; 3F; 4F; 5T; 6F; 7T

Activity 5

١ جنسيّة ٢ تأشيرات ٣ سفارات ٤ مُدير ٥ موظّفون ٦ وُصول ٧ غَرب أوروبا ٨ شَمال إفريقيا ٩ واحدة من ١٠ عَواصِم ١١ مَطلوب ١٢ روما

Activity 6

١b; ٢c; ٣c; ٤a; ٥b

Activity 7

There is a model recording numbered 45 on the audio.

Unit 10

Activity 1

١c; ٢g; ٣b; ٤h; ٥d; ٦a; ٧f; ٨e

Activity 2

١ يوم السَّبت هو يوم <u>السوق</u> في قَرْيَتنا.
٢ اِشْتَرَتْ <u>أختي</u> كيمونو ليمونيّ مَصنوع من <u>الحرير</u>.
٣ سَتَبْحَث خالتي عن <u>مائدة</u> مَصنوعة من <u>الخشب</u>.
٤ سَتَشْتَري أمّي <u>حقيبة</u> رَماديّة يوم <u>السبت</u> القادِم.
٥ تاجِر الكيمونو من <u>الصين</u>. يَبيع الكيمونو بِأ<u>لوان</u> ومقاسات كثيرة.
٦ في السوق، <u>اشتَرَيْتُ</u> خاتِمي المَصنوع مِن الذَّهَب.

Answers to activities

Activity 3
There is a model recording numbered 48 on the audio.

Activity 4
1f; 2h; 3a; 4d; 5b; 6g; 7c; 8e

Activity 5
1 Tuesday.
2 A green cotton hat.
3 It hasn't arrived yet.
4 Yes, he has.
5 Basket number 88T, dated Monday.
6 To go and have breakfast. The delivery is on its way.

Activity 6
1c; 2a; 3c; 4b; 5b; 6a; 7b; 8b

Activity 7
There is a model recording numbered 51 on the audio.

Unit 11

Activity 1
1b; 2c; 3a; 4c; 5b; 6a; 7c; 8b

Activity 2
1d; 2c; 3b; 4f; 5h; 6g; 7e; 8a

Activity 3

١ اِشْتَرَيتُ هذا الخِبز من المخبز.
٢ هذه قَهوَتي. سَأَشْرَبُها الآن.
٣ هَل اِشْتَرَيتَ هذه الخضروات من الخُضَريّ.
٤ شَرِبنا عصير الفواكِه في هذا المحلّ.
٥ اِشْتَرَيتُ هذا السمِك من السمّاك.
٦ دَفَعوا هذا الحِساب لصاحِبة المحلّ.
٧ اِشْتَرَتْ أمّي هذا الشاي من البقّالة.
٨ اِشْتَرى أبي هذه الدِجاجة من اللحّام.

Activity 4
There is a model recording numbered 53 on the audio.

Activity 5

البقّالة	الخضريّ	السمّاك	اللحّام
أسود فِلفِل (black pepper)	بطاطس (potatoes)	٦ سمكات (6 fish)	٦ دجاجات (6 chickens)
أرزّ (rice)	ثوم (garlic)	جَمَبَريّ (prawns)	لحم مفروم (minced meat)
جُبن (cheese)	بصل أحمر (red onions)		
زيت (oil)	ورق عنب (vine leaves)		
حمّص (chick peas)	باذنجان (aubergines)		
زيتون (olives)	طماطم (tomatoes)		
خَلّ (vinegar)	خيار (cucumber)		
زبيب (raisins)	ليمون (lemons)		
زبادي (yoghurt)	جزر (carrots)		
	كرفس (celery)		
	نَعناع (mint)		

Activity 6

١ أتناول إفطاري ٢ واقِفاً ٣ جالِساً على مكتبي ٤ أما عشائي ٥ وَجبة جاهِزة ٦ آكُلها في البيت ٧ المصنوعة من البوليستيرين ٨ مصنوعة من البلاستك

Activity 7

There is a model recording numbered 56 on the audio.

Unit 12

Activity 1

١a؛ ٢c؛ ٣c؛ ٤b؛ ٥c؛ ٦a؛ ٧b

Activity 2

There is a model recording numbered 58 on the audio.

Activity 3

Shukri: I'm <u>Egyptian</u>. I work in a large <u>museum</u>. My name is Shukri.
Zahra: And I'm Zahra. I'm an actress in the <u>theatre</u>.
Shukri: One <u>rainy</u> morning, I met Zahra on the steps of the <u>theatre</u>.
Zahra: I was <u>walking</u> quickly towards the <u>door</u> and he was with his <u>dog</u>, Tito.

Answers to activities

Shukri: I said to her: "Why are you walking quickly when the weather is rainy and the water is everywhere?!".

Zahra: I said to him: "Firstly, let's get aquainted! What's the name of … this beautiful dog?".

Shukri: We laughed, and after that we became friends, me and her and Tito!

Zahra: We both enjoyed walking in the parks and watching films in the cinema.

Shukri: And finally, we got married twenty years ago.

Activity 4

١ (to swim) **f** (swimming); ٢ (to meet) **i** (meeting); ٣ (to head [for]) **j** (heading [for]);

٤ (to drive/to lead) **a** (driving/leading); ٥ (to enjoy) **h** (enjoyment);

٦ (to watch) **c** (watching); ٧ (to smell) **e** (smelling); ٨ (to reserve) **b** (reservation);

٩ (to visit) **d** (visiting); ١٠ (to laugh) **g** (laughing)

Activity 5

1 Always pleasant and sunny.
2 No, he doesn't. (He likes to stay in his country.)
3 To smell the sea breeze and swim in the [resort of] Binzert.
4 To meet Tunisians and to walk amongst them to see their natural [way of] life.
5 To visit the oases and enjoy seeing the palm trees.
6 The old forts.

Activity 6

There is a model recording numbered 61 on the audio.

Unit 13

Activity 1

١b; ٢c; ٣b; ٤c; ٥b; ٦c; ٧a; ٨a; ٩c

Activity 2

١ كلّ يوم، أَصْحو الساعة السابعة والنصف.

٢ بَعدَ ذلك أغسِل وَجهي.

٣ أنظُر من الشبّاك لِأرى حالة الطقس.

٤ عادةً أتَناوَل إفطاري الساعة الثامنة.

٥ أحياناً أَلعَب بَعضَ الرياضة الخفيفة.

٦ أخرُج من البيت الساعة التاسعة والرِبع.

Activity 3

There is a model recording numbered 64 on the audio.

Activity 4

١ أتوجّه نحو ٢ شبّاك الحمّام ٣ حالة الطَّقس ٤ كوب الشاي الأوّل
٥ أُفَكِّر في إفطاري ٦ أي طعام يُقابِلني ٧ إذا كانَ ٨ بَيضة مَسلوقة

Activity 5

1F; 2F; 3T; 4F; 5F; 6T; 7T; 8F

Activity 6

There is an open-ended writing activity. The commentary will depend on your own evening routine. Try to show your finished piece to an Arabic speaker.

Unit 14

Activity 1

١ (king) **c** (kings); ٢ (government) **f** (governments); ٣ (minister) **e** (ministers);

٤ (feast/festival) **h** (feasts/festivals); ٥ (people/populace) **g** (peoples/populaces);

٦ (industry) **a** (industries); ٧ (religion) **b** (religions); ٨ (society) **d** (societies)

Activity 2

There is a model recording numbered 67 on the audio.

Activity 3

1 the economy
2 public holiday
3 visiting dignitaries
4 general inspiration

Activity 4

1 Special <u>thanks</u> to the Minister of the <u>Economy</u> who has <u>helped</u> me. Our <u>economy</u> is strong and is growing every <u>day</u>!
2 Happy <u>Eid/feast</u> on the occasion of <u>National</u> Day. <u>Health</u> and <u>happiness</u> to all the <u>people</u>!
3 I <u>received</u> a group of <u>princes</u> today. The <u>future</u> is bright for <u>everyone</u>!
4 The <u>government</u> is working for <u>you</u> seven <u>days</u> a week. Together we will <u>build</u> a better <u>life</u>!

Activity 5

١ قانونيّ ٢ اِقتِصاديّ ٣ ثَقافيّ ٤ دينيّ ٥ صِناعيّ
٦ تَقليديّ ٧ شَعبيّ ٨ صِحّيّ ٩ عَقليّ

Answers to activities

Activity 6
Messages 1, 3 and 5.

Activity 7
١b; ٢c; ٣c; ٤a; ٥b; ٦a

Activity 8
This is an open-ended writing activity. The slogans and posters will depend on your imagination and preferences. Try to show your finished piece to an Arabic speaker.